Fast-Piece Appliqué
Easy, Artful Quilts by Machine

Rose Hughes

Martingale®
Create with Confidence

Fast-Piece Appliqué: Easy, Artful Quilts by Machine
© 2015 by Rose Hughes

Martingale®
19021 120th Ave. NE, Ste. 102
Bothell, WA 98011-9511 USA
ShopMartingale.com

Printed in China
20 19 18 17 16 15   8 7 6 5 4 3 2 1

**Library of Congress Cataloging-in-Publication
Data is available upon request.**

ISBN: 978-1-60468-469-8

Mission Statement

Dedicated to providing quality products and
service to inspire creativity.

Credits

PUBLISHER AND CHIEF VISIONARY OFFICER:
    Jennifer Erbe Keltner

EDITOR IN CHIEF: Mary V. Green

DESIGN DIRECTOR: Paula Schlosser

MANAGING EDITOR: Karen Costello Soltys

ACQUISITIONS EDITOR: Karen M. Burns

TECHNICAL EDITOR: Laurie Baker

COPY EDITOR: Tiffany Mottet

PRODUCTION MANAGER: Regina Girard

COVER AND INTERIOR DESIGNER: Connor Chin

PHOTOGRAPHER: Brent Kane

ILLUSTRATOR: Rose Wright

Contents

Bonus projects online! Visit www.ShopMartingale.com/extras to download two free bonus patterns, "Scrap Happy Holiday Trees" and "Scrap Happy Pillow."

Introduction

It's funny how what once was often comes roaring back again, sometimes with very few changes. Anyone who was around in the 1970s will probably agree with me when I say I know that all the platform shoes I've seen lately must have been tucked away in some dusty old warehouse just waiting to be found—they look so much like the shoes I remember!

It feels like the same thing is happening with my quilting. When I started quilting, I fell in love with Amish-style quilts. I loved the graphic, wonderfully large designs and how the Amish used solid colors in ways that made you sit up and take notice. If this wasn't enough, the quilting in those Amish wonders was exquisite and worked in designs that were beautifully juxtaposed with the quilt pattern. As my stitching life continued and my own quilting style took shape, it no longer mimicked the Amish, but the love of those quilts definitely stuck with me and influences me every day.

Now, back to the present. Are you scratching your head and thinking, "How do those platform shoes relate to quilting?" A lot of the quilts being made today remind me of those earlier quilts, but luckily no one just pulled them out of a dusty warehouse. Today's quilts bring back those wonderfully large, graphic designs, and the quilted line has made an incredible transformation. While the stitching of today is beautifully added to create incredible quilts, it's being done in new ways with new threads in order to make its own statement.

In this book, I'm sharing with you some basic ideas on simplifying things from our daily lives and turning them into large, simple, graphic designs. I'll also show you several ways to utilize my Fast-Piece Appliqué technique to help you stitch designs of any style. If you're not familiar with this technique, I give instructions for it and several variations in "Construction Techniques" on page 16. These construction options will let you fully take advantage of the wonderful new quilting possibilities available to us lucky quilters today.

 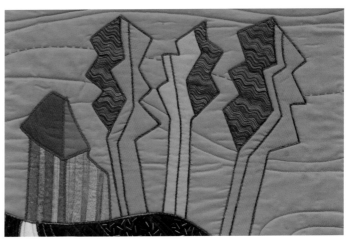

Simplify, Simplify, Simplify

We all have our own way of seeing the world around us, and unless you want to produce a totally realistic design, you'll need to learn what part of the realistic image is important so you can begin to eliminate unnecessary detail. The choices we make—what to keep or what to eliminate—allow us to use our creativity, our imaginations. Through our choices, we put our own personal stamp on an image and also encourage our viewers to use their imaginations, too. Most of us do this automatically, and we often don't realize we're eliminating unnecessary detail from an image we're simplifying. There are other times when there is so much detail that we don't know where to start.

Simplifying is an important skill and, with a little practice, you can turn out some really wonderful designs that you can't wait to turn into quilts. Some people believe that to simplify you must give up everything, but really it's about keeping the right shape in the right size in the right place in order to recall or imply the original image to your mind. You're creating a visual surprise, because each of us is different and each person simplifies differently. Give this a try with the following exercises.

Lesson 1

When you begin to simplify an item or scene, you begin making personal selections. You'll begin to emphasize one element over another, and you'll begin creating a design that takes on your personality. You can simplify an item yet have it maintain its original character, or you can continue modifying the item until its original character is beyond recognition.

Below is a photo of an oak leaf that has started turning into its autumn colors. The illustrations that follow show how I modified the basic shape.

Here's my first line drawing, capturing the leaf's basic shape.

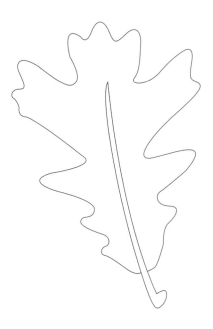

In this first set of simplified drawings, I modified and simplified the leaf's basic shape while maintaining the basic character of the original.

The drawings in this set show the beginnings of liberties being taken, and already it's difficult to recognize the original leaf that inspired these designs.

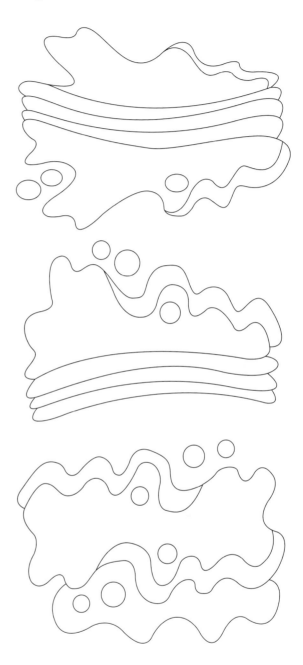

Lesson 2

In my Fast-Piece Appliqué workshops over the years, I begin with a "shape" test, which is just a fun new-age personality test that gets everyone thinking about basic shapes. After all, quilting is all about fabric shapes being stitched together. Details can be added later through quilting or embellishment, or you can leave the shape clear of details.

Think about these questions as you look at the photos below:

▌ What central idea or theme is called to mind when you look at each photo?

▌ Which lines are necessary to identify the shapes needed to portray your idea?

▌ Are there lines or shapes needed to create a sense of depth?

▌ Are there lines or shapes needed to maintain the appearance of an underlying structure?

▌ Where there is a large grouping of one thing, which shapes are the most important to convey your theme?

Once you've answered these basic questions, pull out some sketch paper and try drawing your newly simplified images.

I admit it—I'm a collector. I collect ideas, words, pictures, and all sorts of things that give me inspiration or set off a spark. Some are small enough to take home in a pocket and set on a shelf or pin to a wall. Others are too big so I must record them in some way that, when I look at my recording, the spark is rekindled. I always carry a sketchbook with me for these big recordings.

This sketchbook isn't a pretty thing, just a small book with blank pages that's easy to take along. I've filled many, many of these little books over the years, and they have a shelf of honor in my studio. I just never know what might jump out at me when I look back over the pages.

These "sketchy" little books are not art journals. They're not filled with beautiful, inviting, thought-provoking pages created with mixed-media materials. They are filled with words and little pencil drawings. And because my sketchbook just might be the only paper I have with me, you might find a website address, a friend's phone number, or directions to that wonderful little restaurant I visited when traveling.

I believe we should all carry sketchbooks and, of course, a couple of pencils, because you never know where the day may take you.

Essentials

One of the things I love about being a quilter is the multitude of ways there are to work with fabric, to stitch our ideas, and to create just the look we're seeking. In this chapter, you'll find a list of basic supplies, information on tool selection, and instructions for the various construction methods used throughout the book. My hope is that you'll try these methods and enjoy one or more enough to use them not only for the projects in this book, but for future projects as well.

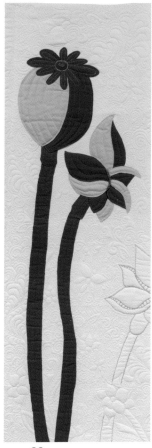

page 33

page 55

page 67

Supplies

Boy, we're lucky quilters. We're living in a time when there's an entire industry devoted to coming up with amazing tools and materials for making us happy. Choosing just the right item can be somewhat daunting though, so in this section I'll give some ideas on how to choose the right stuff.

Fabric

Have you ever seen a quilt that pulls at your heart strings or has created a wonderful, exciting place that makes you want to jump in and be part of the scene? The quilts that affect you in this way have effectively created a mood. Of all the materials you'll be gathering, the fabric you select sets the mood for the whole quilt.

The traditional cottons used for quilts are available in many colors, textures, and fun prints, but for the quilts in this book, you aren't limited to just quilting cottons. Expand your selections to include non-traditional fabrics as well. Keep in mind that for any other fabric besides cotton, you'll want to ensure that it can be ironed without incident before using it in any project. Additionally, silk and other lightweight fabrics that are prone to raveling should be stabilized with fusible interfacing to eliminate slipping or fraying.

Color Choices

Artists use many technigues to establish a mood in their work. Subject matter and scenery in large part set the mood, but color can control it all. Blues are cool and soothing. Reds are wild, hot, and crazy. Yellow can make you feel happy, and it's said that orange is the color of conversation.

It's important to learn the basic properties and theories of color so that you can use color effectively. The colors represented on the basic color wheel are pure, bright colors known as hues. Once these hues are combined with white, they're lighter and are called tints. By combining hues with black, they become darker and are referred to as shades.

The most important hues are yellow, red, and blue. They are the *primary colors,* and using them in certain combinations creates the other hues on the color wheel.

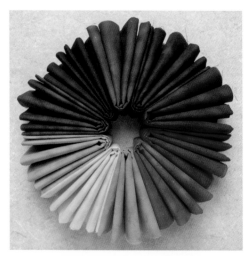

Fabrics are the quilt artist's palette and there's no limit to the effects that can be achieved. Here the basic color wheel is expressed in fabrics.

Secondary colors are created when two primary colors are mixed in equal amounts. Green is the mixture of yellow and blue, violet is the mixture of blue and red, and orange is the mixture of red and yellow. On the wheel, each of these colors is exactly midway between two primary colors.

Tertiary colors lie between primary and secondary colors and are a mixture of those colors. There are six tertiary colors: yellow-green, blue-green, blue-violet, red-violet, red-orange, and yellow-orange.

The terms *monochromatic, analogous,* and *complementary* are used when describing basic combinations of hues, tints, and shades. They work to create certain consistent effects that are known as schemes and should be considered when selecting fabrics. Colors working together help support the mood you want to create, and by selecting your fabrics based on a particular color scheme, you'll easily create the mood you want in your quilt.

The *monochromatic scheme* uses one color and any tint or shade of the selected color. This generally creates a serene feeling, but the right combinations can also be dramatic. Selectively using black and/or white in the monochromatic scheme helps add interest, like what you might see created in the dark shadows of a doorway or the bright highlights of a sunny afternoon.

All the colors used in a monochromatic color scheme come from the same color family.

An *analogous color scheme* creates a beautiful and harmonious feeling. This is accomplished by choosing three colors adjacent to one another on the color wheel. They're part of the same family and contain a little bit of each other, so how could they not work well? Great examples of analogous color schemes can be seen all around us. The next time you take a walk through a park or along the beach and feel calm, note the colors around you. Chances are you're surrounded by analogous colors.

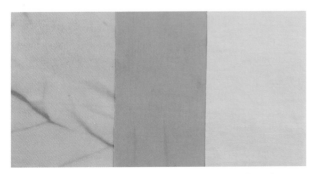

Using green, blue-green, and yellow-green together shows how harmony is accomplished by using an analogous color scheme.

If you want a lot of color contrast, or "pop," then you'll want to use a *complementary color scheme.* This scheme gets its excitement by choosing colors directly opposite each other on the color wheel. Opposites attract and, when placed together, can also cause sparks to fly! That calm you felt when walking through an analogous color scheme can change completely when you come across some wild red-violet flowers among the yellow-green foliage.

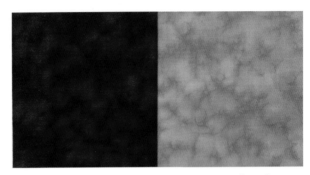

Going for excitement? Use a complementary color scheme such as this red-violet and yellow-green fabric combination.

Learning about color mechanics is important, but observation is the most valuable tool in gaining an understanding of color. Observe nature and the life around you. Pay attention to color. Where it shows up may surprise you, as will the way in which just a small amount can change the feeling of a whole scene.

Once you've decided on the mood and some basic colors, you'll want to give yourself lots of options. Start pulling as many fabrics from your stash as you think might work well together, but keep in mind there's more to fabric selection than just color. The fabrics you select can provide pattern, line, shape, texture, movement, and a sense of scale as well. All these design elements help you create a mood, so let's take a closer look at them.

Texture

Have you ever had the urge to touch a quilt you saw hanging in a show? I know you have. We all have. Texture is inviting. It creates depth and visual interest. Fabrics may give a feeling that a surface is smooth or rough. This is sometimes conveyed by the physical characteristics of the fabrics themselves, like silks or brocades. It can also be conveyed by patterns of rhythmically repeating motifs, or open areas printed in variegated colors. These types of fabrics seem to invite you to run your hand over them to feel the subtle variations.

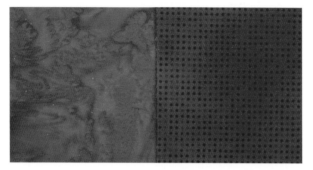

Textural fabrics invite you to touch and experience a quilt by giving the sense that a surface is smooth or rough.

Line

Movement and direction are important design elements, and line works to create movement. Horizontal, vertical, and diagonal lines all imply action and direction. Lines can be thick or thin, curvy or sharply angled; each one conveys a different emotion or feeling. Additionally, lines can define shapes and help establish boundaries, and they can also be a connecting element. How do lines or stripes in your fabrics help express the mood you're trying to communicate? Do the lines pull you into the quilt, or do they draw your eyes away from your design?

Different types of lines can create different moods. Can you envision how these lines would bring attention to your quilt?

Contrast

Remember, color doesn't work on its own. It's always working together with the other colors around it, no matter how large or small those areas of color are. Contrast contributes excitement, creates tension, and relieves monotony. Light to dark or dark to light, contrast is the study of opposites that can be brought about by a difference in value or a difference in hue, and can be either low-key or highly charged choices. As you select your fabrics, remember that the main area of contrast may be between the fabrics and the embellishments. Be careful that the stage dressings don't detract attention from your main characters.

High contrast between light and dark fabrics helps separate one area from another.

Repetition

The eye naturally searches for similarities. Placing the same color or print in various places within the quilt will cause the viewer's eyes to travel, creating interest and movement that draw the viewer's attention throughout the work.

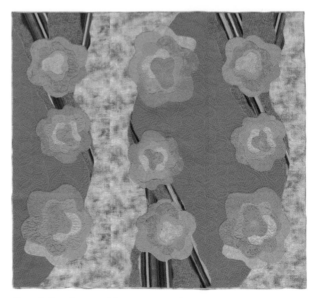

Six solid and print fabrics are used in various positions in each of the roses on this quilt and provide a good example of repetition.

BASIC SEWING KIT

Have the following supplies on hand anytime you're working on a project.

For Drawing and Marking
Soft-lead pencil
Pencil eraser
Fine-line (not ultrafine) permanent black marker
Chalk powder or cartridge-type marker (optional)
Fabric markers (optional)

For Cutting
Paper scissors
Fabric scissors
Duckbill appliqué scissors
Rotary cutter and cutting mat
Long ruler

For Fabric Preparation
Light- to medium-weight paper-backed fusible web
Featherweight to lightweight fusible interfacing

For Machine Sewing
Size 80/12 or 90/14 topstitching or metallic sewing-machine needles
Size 100 topstitching sewing-machine needle

For Pressing
Iron
Ironing board
Pressing sheet (to protect ironing surfaces when using fusible products)

For Basting
Lightweight cotton or cotton-blend batting
Masking tape
Safety pins (or product required for your favorite basting method)

For Hand Dimensional Stitching and Beading
Size 2 crewel hand-sewing needles
Size 10 or 11 Sharps hand-sewing needles
Needle threader (optional)
Thimble (optional)
Small pincushion
Beading cup/tray

My basic hand-stitching tool kit

Freezer Paper

Freezer paper is essential to the Fast-Piece Appliqué process where you'll use machine piecing and appliqué techniques in controlled combination. It's delightfully paradoxical; the real secret to achieving a curving and flowing line is to freeze it by using freezer paper. Freezer paper is first used to create the curved pattern and then to hold the fabric pieces in place with a very high level of accuracy as they are quickly and easily sewn together by machine. In this way, fabric grain will be kept consistent throughout the sewing process, and there will be no need for pins. Easing curves will become a thing of the past. You can find freezer paper in most grocery stores and some quilt shops. Freezer paper is white paper with one smooth side and that's easy to write on and an opposite side that's coated with plastic. It's available in 15"-, 18"-, and 24"-wide rolls and sheets.

Sewing Machine

For the projects in this book, use a sewing machine that you're familiar with and that has zigzag and machine-quilting capabilities. Make sure that it's in good working order and that you know how to change the length and width of the stitches. In addition to a standard or ¼" presser foot for straight stitching, you'll need a foot that accommodates wide zigzag stitching for couching yarn. Check with your sewing-machine dealer for a foot designed to couch yarn easily, such as a braiding foot, couching foot, pearl beading foot, or cording foot. You may also want a darning or quilting foot for optional machine quilting.

Machine-Sewing Threads and Glue

You'll need several different types of thread for the machine-stitching process. Threads for hand stitching are covered in "Hand-Stitching Threads" at right.

Sewing thread. Select a 40-weight cotton thread in a neutral color, such as gray or beige, for general Fast-Piece Appliqué construction. Clear monofilament thread can be used when you don't want your stitches to show. I use it for the "Fused-Fabric Elements" (page 20) and "Invisible Thread Variation" (page 19) techniques. Water-soluble thread is also an option for constructing projects when a more three-dimensional look is desired (refer to "Wash-Away Construction Variations" on page 20).

Decorative thread. Quilting and couching play big roles in the final look of your piece, and choosing a great thread is the first step to success. Select from the wide variety of options available, including metallic, silk, rayon, and even wool. Mix them up and have fun!

Bobbin thread. Select a thread that works well with your top thread, noting that it will be visible on the back of the quilt. In most cases, my choice is clear monofilament.

Washable glue. Like water-soluble thread, non-permanent glue is an option for constructing projects when you want to give the raw edges of the fabric pieces a chance to fluff up.

From cotton to rayon to metallic and beyond, there are many amazing thread choices for machine quilting and couching.

Hand-Stitching Threads

Accessorize and embellish your quilt with hand quilting and beading. Each require different threads.

Embroidery floss. This decorative thread is composed of six very loosely twisted strands that make the floss highly versatile. The six strands can be used together, or they can be easily separated so you can use just one or two at a time. Or combine different colored strands for blended effects. Embroidery floss is generally available by the skein, in cotton, silk, and rayon, and can be found in a wide range of solid and variegated colors.

Pearl cotton. This is another type of decorative thread that can be used for dimensional stitching, but unlike embroidery floss, it's tightly twisted and not divisible. Pearl cotton comes generally in either skeins or balls. The four most common sizes are 12 (very fine), 8 (fine), 5 (medium), and 3 (heavy).

Beading thread. Use an exceptionally strong but pliable thread in a color that matches the fabric where the beads will be attached. My favorite beading thread is a 60-weight lint-free polyester.

Some of my favorite hand-stitching threads—ready to be needled up and stitched into my next project

Yarns

Yarns are used to cover seams and outline shapes. There is a tempting array of colors, weights, and textures available, so you can have lots of fun shopping for and playing with them. Audition yarns by laying them on your quilt, selecting by color first, and then by thickness and texture. Make sure the yarn is thick enough to adequately cover your stitching line. Consider combining multiple thinner strands to supply the needed coverage *and* provide a great look.

Yarn is another one of those materials that's hard to resist. Here are just a few of my favorites!

Beads

Beads are the perfect accessory for your quilts! These small wonders come in a variety of sizes, shapes, and colors, as well as many natural and manufactured materials—glass, wood, stone, and ceramic, just to name a few.

When selecting beads, it's important to consider how they'll lie on your quilt. In most instances, you won't want to use large, bulky beads that will create a big bump in your work and keep it from lying flat. Don't worry though, because there are loads of beads out there that will lie flat on your quilt. You can find them by canvassing local bead stores, checking out bead retailers while traveling, or browsing the many online stores. Some my favorite beads for adding sparkle, direction, texture, and dimension include seed beads, small glass squares, and bugle beads. Mixing them all together makes it easy and fun to create depth and interest within your quilt.

I love to mix beads so much that I have my own line! My mixes provide a nice assortment of beads that will lie flat and are easy to stitch to any project.

Interfacing

Whether you're using silk, a fabric that frays easily, or you need to give a project a bit more shape and support, interfacing is your friend. It's been used in garment construction for a long time, customarily as an extra textile layer in collars, cuffs, necklines, and pockets. There are two basic types: sew-in and fusible. Fusible is the best choice for our use.

Interfacings come in a variety of weights and stiffness to suit different purposes. A very lightweight interfacing works well on silk to set the threads so they won't fray. HeatnBond featherweight fusible interfacing is my favorite for using on silk.

Once you've selected the best interfacing for your needs, follow the manufacturer's instructions to fuse it to the wrong side of the fabric, prior to cutting the pattern pieces for your project.

Construction Techniques

Fast-Piece Appliqué construction has become an old friend over the years, allowing me to stitch together almost any design I can dream up. Just like in a piecing project, each shape is cut from a separate fabric, and then, using elements of appliqué, this technique enables you to make easy work of stitching curves, circles, and just about any shape you can imagine.

In this section, I've included the original method for stitching the quilt top together, as well as new variations. With these stitching options, you can achieve a variety of looks and open up more opportunities for long-arm quilting and finishing.

Enlarging the Pattern Design

All the patterns for the projects in this book need to be enlarged to create the finished size shown. There are many ways to enlarge a pattern; this section covers instructions for a few of these methods. You can also use these methods for any design you create on your own.

Grid Method

The grid method is a quick and simple way to enlarge a pattern by hand. You'll need a pencil, a piece of tracing paper slightly larger than the size of the pattern in this book, and a piece of tracing paper the finished size of the quilt or panel.

1. Trace the pattern from the book onto the smaller piece of tracing paper. Cut out the pattern on the outer line.

2. Fold the pattern in half vertically, and then fold it in half vertically again.

3. Unfold the pattern, and then fold it in half horizontally. Fold it in half horizontally again. Unfold the pattern. The fold lines have created a grid.

4. Repeat the folding process with the larger piece of tracing paper. When both papers are unfolded, you'll have the same number of grid lines on both papers.

5. Now, look at one section of the grid on the smaller piece of paper, and draw what you see in the corresponding section of the grid on the larger piece of paper. I start at the top left section of the pattern, and after the first section is enlarged I go on to the next section, working left to right and top to bottom until everything is enlarged. If there are changes or corrections, I make them with pencil at this point.

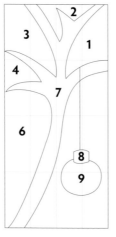

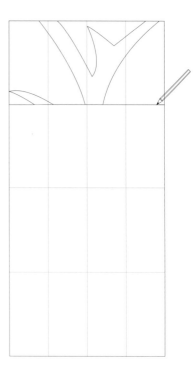

Scanner and Computer

For this method, you'll need to scan the pattern into an image-editing program. After enlarging the pattern on your computer, print it out as a tiled image. The tiled pieces can be reassembled into a full-sized pattern.

Opaque Projector

Place the original pattern under a projector unit and project it onto a larger piece of tracing paper taped to a wall. Each type of projector has its own requirements regarding the use of special transparency films, as well as size limitations of the originals used.

Local Copy Center

Most copy centers can enlarge your pattern for you. Make sure you provide the associate with the percentage indicated in the instructions so they can enlarge the pattern appropriately.

Fast-Piece Appliqué Basics

These step-by-step instructions will guide you through the basic process of the Fast-Piece Appliqué method.

Prepare the Freezer-Paper Templates

1. Using the desired method, enlarge the patterns for your project the percentage indicated in the instructions. The enlarged patterns will be used to make the freezer-paper patterns and also as placement guides.

2. For each panel, cut a piece of freezer paper the same size as your enlarged design. In most of the projects in this book, you'll need to combine several sheets to create a piece large enough to trace the complete pattern. The trick is to join the pieces securely and in a way that can be ironed without worrying about burning tape or glue. Overlap the freezer-paper pieces 1". Using double-stick tape or a glue stick, apply adhesive between the overlapped layers and press the pieces together with your fingers. Some long-time users of the Fast-Piece Appliqué method have found that stitching the papers together also works well.

3. Place a joined piece of freezer paper over one of the enlarged paper patterns, shiny side down.

4. Using a permanent marker, trace the lines and numbers onto the freezer paper. Add hash marks (short lines drawn across the pattern lines) along the lines between the numbered pieces. These marks will be used to match the pieces and sew them together after the freezer-paper pattern has been cut apart to make the templates.

Make a hash mark across the lines between numbered shapes.

5. Repeat steps 3 and 4 with the remaining panels.

Select and Mark the Fabrics

After freezer-paper patterns are completed, the fun begins. Now you need to select a fabric for each numbered pattern piece of the quilt top. As each fabric is selected, it's best to mark the fabric with its corresponding pattern-piece number. I use numbered pieces of masking tape.

1. Lay out a strip of masking tape on your cutting mat.

2. With a marker, write a number on the tape for each of the pattern shapes. For example, if there are six shapes, mark the numbers 1–6 on the tape.

3. With your rotary cutter, cut apart the tape between the numbers.

4. Select a fabric for piece 1 on your pattern, and then place the tape marker for piece 1 on the fabric. Repeat this process with the remaining pieces and numbers.

Prepare the Fabric and Pattern Pieces for Sewing

Once you've selected the fabrics, prepare each of the various pattern pieces for sewing.

1. Cut apart the freezer-paper patterns by cutting directly on the lines between the shapes.

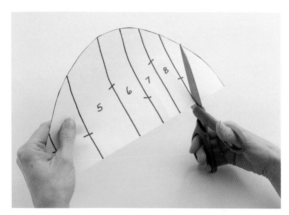

Cut apart freezer-paper patterns to make templates.

2. Iron each template, shiny side down, onto the right side of the corresponding numbered fabric. Be sure to remove the masking-tape number before ironing the template in place!

3. Cut out each fabric piece, leaving ½" extra around the template for seam allowance.

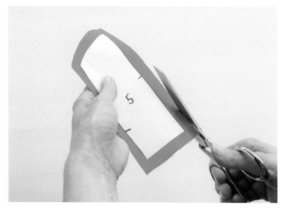

Cut each fabric piece ½" larger than template.

Construct the Quilt Top

Set your sewing machine for straight stitching. Use a neutral thread on the top and in the bobbin.

1. Select two fabric pieces adjacent to each other in the pattern. The instructions for each project will give you the assembly order.

2. Place the pieces side by side on your ironing board. Butt the edges of the templates together using the hash marks for alignment. To do this, you'll need to lift up one freezer-paper edge and slide the seam allowance of the other fabric piece under it (see "Light and Dark Fabric" on page 19).

3. Once the pieces are lined up, slightly separate them, leaving only the width of a sewing-machine needle between the edges of the two templates. Iron the freezer-paper templates back into place.

Lift the template edge of one piece and slide the seam allowance of the other piece under it. Once aligned, press pieces in place.

4. Following the pattern pieces, sew in the space between the two shapes.

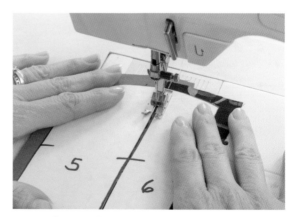

Sew in the space between the two templates.

Light and Dark Fabric

When joining a very light fabric to a dark one, lift the freezer-paper template from the light fabric and slide the seam allowance of the dark fabric on top of it. This will eliminate any shadows that could possibly be seen through the light fabric.

5. After sewing the two pieces together, lift up the edge of the freezer-paper template from the fabric that's on the bottom, exposing the stitching line and the raw edge of the fabric that's on top. Lift only enough to allow for trimming the excess fabric.

6. Trim the excess top fabric as close to the stitching line as possible using duckbill appliqué scissors. Trim only along the stitching line on top. Once the fabric is trimmed, iron the freezer paper back into place.

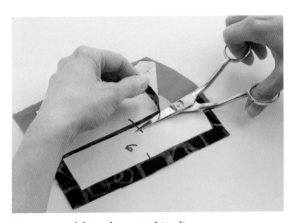

Trim excess fabric along stitching line.

7. Continue sewing pattern pieces together in this manner to create sections. Sew the sections together in the same manner to complete the top. Leave the templates in place.

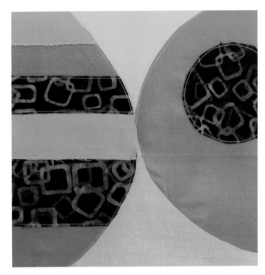

Curved pieces come together easily using the Fast-Piece Appliqué method. Here, the templates have been removed to show that a neutral thread was used for construction.

Invisible Thread Variation

Fast-Piece Appliqué is a raw-edge construction method. Using the basic method, stitching lines are somewhat visible, depending on your fabrics and thread. If you want a completely unobstructed canvas on which to embellish your quilt top, follow the basic method but use a clear monofilament thread in the top and bobbin to stitch the pieces together.

Invisible thread was used to Fast-Piece Appliqué this block. Compare it to the block above, which used a neutral thread for construction.

Wash-Away Construction Variations

It might seem crazy to use a wash-away product to construct your quilt top, but it produces fun frayed edges that add to the embellishment of the quilt while also creating a wonderful canvas for machine quilting. Just keep in mind that you'll be washing the quilt once it's completely finished (layered, quilted, bound, and embellished), so it's important to start with prewashed fabrics.

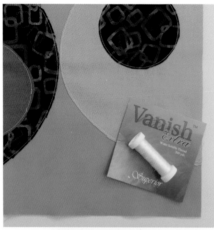

Use the basic Fast-Piece Appliqué technique and water-soluble thread (top) or glue (bottom) to construct your projects.

Water-Soluble Thread Option

Simply use water-soluble thread to construct your quilt top, following the instructions in "Fast-Piece Appliqué Basics" on page 17.

Glue Option

This option involves using white, washable glue in an applicator bottle with a very narrow opening. There's no sewing required; it's done without ever taking a stitch!

1. Follow the instructions in "Fast-Piece Appliqué Basics" on page 17 through step 2 of "Construct the Quilt Top."

2. With your pattern templates lined up, turn over the fabric pieces to the wrong side. Lift up the fabric on top and apply a very light line or small beads of glue to the edge. Press the edge back in place with your fingers, and then press it with a warm iron.

Apply glue to fabric edge and press in place.

3. Turn the pieces over to the right side (freezer-paper side). Lift up the edge of the freezer-paper template from the fabric that is on the bottom, exposing the seam allowance of the fabric that is on top. Trim the excess top fabric as close to the freezer-paper template as possible. Iron the freezer-paper template back in place.

Trim excess seam allowance from top fabric.

Fused-Fabric Elements

Light- to medium-weight paper-backed fusible web was used for several projects in this book to create motifs that stand out from the background. The raised elements are created by fusing the decorative top fabric to a backing fabric. The backing fabric isn't likely to be seen once the piece is stitched in place, so it doesn't really matter what fabric you use. I usually use the same fabric as I've used for the top or a solid-color fabric. Once the top and backing fabrics are fused together and the shape is cut out, the fused motif is placed on the background and stitched down.

Fused appliqués stand out slightly from the background because of the extra layer of fabric.

1. Iron the top and backing fabrics to remove any wrinkles.

2. Follow the manufacturer's instructions to fuse the web to the wrong side of the top fabric. Let it cool, and then remove the paper backing.

3. Lay the fusible side of the top fabric against the wrong side of the backing fabric, and fuse them together.

4. Place your freezer-paper template, shiny side down, on the top fabric and press it in place with the iron. Cut out the shape, cutting directly next to the template. Remove the freezer-paper template.

Press the freezer-paper template onto the fused fabric and cut out the shape.

5. Referring to the enlarged paper pattern for placement, place the fused shape on the background piece. Use masking tape along the edges to hold it in place. Using masking tape rather than pins to hold the fused piece in place keeps everything flat without creating bulk or bunching.

6. With matching or invisible thread and a straight stitch, stitch around the edge of the piece, removing the tape pieces as you come to them.

Tape the fused appliqué in place and stitch around the edges.

Creating Fused Appliqué Units

When you have multiple pieces making up one larger unit, like the seedpods in "Poppy Pods" (page 33), it's possible to create a cleaner, more unified appearance if you create an appliqué unit, rather than fusing each element separately.

1. Cut out each of the top pieces and place them together on the fusible side of the backing fabric as they will be joined in the final unit.

2. Cover the pieces with a Teflon pressing sheet, or the protective paper from the fusible web, and fuse the pieces to the backing fabric.

3. Let the unit cool, and then cut it out.

Set-In Pieces

Stitching one shape to another so the shape on top appears to be coming from the middle of the bottom shape can seem challenging. We call these *set-in pieces*. Follow these simple steps to see how Fast-Piece Appliqué makes easy work of set-in shapes.

In this sample, the smaller circles were set into the larger circles.

1. Identify the prepared fabric pieces that require set-in stitching and place them on the ironing board. There will be an outer piece with an opening in the freezer paper and an inner piece that will fit into the opening of the freezer paper.

Compound Set-In Units

Create more texture and interest in your set-in pieces by cutting them from a piece of patchwork. This might be just the place to use leftovers from strip sets or small orphan blocks. The roofs of the houses in "Gone Fruity for Meadow Orchards" (page 63) and "Sun's Up" (page 67) were created with pieced fabrics.

2. Gently lift off the freezer paper from the outer fabric piece until there is adequate space to slide the inner fabric piece under the opening.

3. Slide the inner piece, right side up, between the outer-piece template and fabric until the outer and inner freezer-paper templates are aligned. Iron the outer freezer-paper template back in place.

Slide the inner piece between the outer template and fabric pieces.

4. Gently remove the inner freezer-paper pattern and press the unit again.

5. Stitch just inside the opening of the outer freezer-paper template.

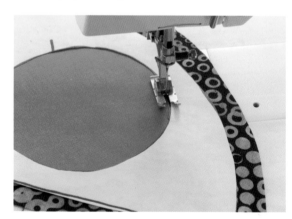

Stitch just inside the opening edge.

6. Once stitched, lift the freezer paper and trim the inset fabric seam allowance to the stitching line.

Set-On Pieces

Using the set-on construction method, you can pre-assemble large sections of the full quilt design, and then stitch the completed units in place on the background. These step-by-step instructions show you how to prepare the pattern pieces for set-on stitching.

The small circles in this sample have been stitched to the larger half circles, and then the half circles have been set on and stitched to the background fabric.

1. Prepare individual templates and fabric pieces as described in "Fast-Piece Appliqué Basics" on page 17.
2. Join pieces to form a complete appliqué unit using your preferred construction method. Leave the freezer-paper templates in place.

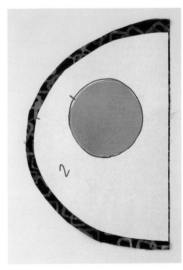

These pieces have been stitched together to form a unit.

3. Once the unit is complete, refer to the full-sized pattern as a guide to place it on the background. Use masking tape to secure it in place.
4. Straight stitch around the outside of the joined unit using the edge of the freezer-paper template as a guide, removing the masking tape just before stitching over it.

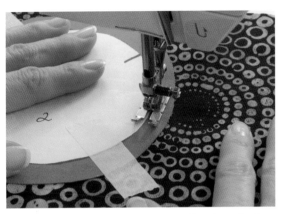

Tape the joined unit to the background and stitch along the edge of the template to secure it.

5. Remove the freezer-paper templates and trim the outermost fabrics to the stitching line.

Paper Piecing

Paper (or foundation) piecing makes fast, accurate work of achieving sharp points and straight lines. This technique is done by placing fabrics onto a paper foundation and sewing on the marked lines. The "striped" pieces in "Seedpod Polka" (page 59) were constructed this way.

Fabrics were paper pieced together to create the striped appliqué on the left.

1. Trace or photocopy the paper-piecing patterns for your project onto foundation paper. Special papers are available specifically for foundation piecing or you can use any paper that you can see through and tear away easily. Include the numbers that are shown on each section of the pattern, and leave an additional ½" beyond the outside edges of the complete pattern for seam allowance.

2. Cut a piece of fabric for each numbered section of the pattern, making sure it's at least ½" larger on all sides than the section. Once you've cut all the pieces, lay them out on the full-sized paper pattern guide.

3. With the foundation pattern right side up, place the fabric for section 1 right side up on section 1 of the paper foundation, making sure at least ½" of fabric extends beyond all sides. Lay the fabric piece for section 2 on top of the section 1 fabric, right sides together, and pin both fabrics in place through the middle of section 1. Check from the wrong side to make sure the fabric from section 1 extends at least ½" on all sides of section 1, as shown below. Make sure the section 2 fabric is positioned so it will cover all of section 2 when pressed into place, again with at least ½" extending on all sides. Test this by pinning on the line between sections 1 and 2 and then flipping the fabric over section 2.

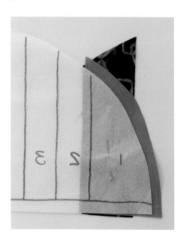

Pin fabric pieces for sections 1 and 2 to section 1 of the pattern. Check from the wrong side to make sure the fabric for section 1 extends at least ½" on all sides of section 1.

4. From the wrong side of the foundation paper, stitch on the line between sections 1 and 2. Remove the pin and then press fabric piece 2 over section 2, making sure it extends at least ½" on all sides. If the section is adequately covered, trim the seam allowances to ¼".

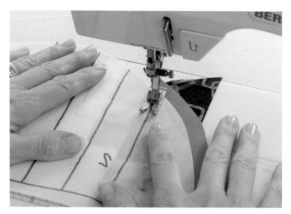

Stitch on the marked line of the pattern between sections 1 and 2.

5. Repeat the process to place, pin, stitch, and press the remaining fabric pieces to the foundation in numerical order.

Finishing Details

For me, the fun begins when the quilt top is completed. Now I can start choosing the types of embellishments I want to use to show off the design. This may include couching, dimensional stitching, and quilting with thread or beads. In this section, I'll review the details you need to pull your quilt top all together into the finished piece you envision. Begin by layering the quilt top with batting and backing.

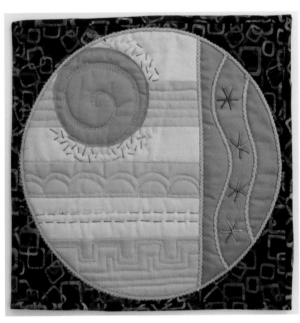

Here is a sample of some of my favorite fun finishes.

Preparing the Quilt Sandwich

1. Iron the backing fabric and lay it right side down on a flat surface. Use masking tape along the edges to secure it in place.

2. Center the batting on the backing and tape it in place.

3. Carefully remove the freezer-paper templates from the quilt top. Press the quilt top.

4. Center the quilt top on the batting, right side up, and then tape it in place.

5. Baste the layers together by inserting safety pins every few inches.

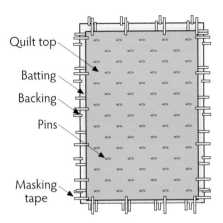

Couching

Once the quilt sandwich has been pin basted, you can choose to couch yarn along all the raw edges of the quilt design to cover up the stitching lines and to delineate the shapes, or you can leave the raw edges untreated so they'll fray. If you choose to couch the seam lines, use an open-toe or braiding foot on your sewing machine.

1. Select yarns for couching that coordinate with your quilt-top fabrics.

2. Thread the sewing machine needle with a decorative thread, such as metallic, decorative cotton blend, or rayon, that will work with the yarns you're planning to use. Wind the bobbin with a thread that's compatible with the top thread and that will look nice on the back of the quilt.

3. Feed the selected yarn through the foot opening. If you're using an open-toe foot, hold the yarn in place below the opening.

4. Set your machine for a zigzag stitch. Set the stitch length to zero and the width to 3 or 3.5 mm.

5. Start sewing at the end of a seam line and take about four stitches in place to lock the stitch.

6. Reset the stitch length to 3.5 mm. Continue stitching, couching the yarn over the seam line so it covers the raw edges of the fabric and the stitching line. Remove any safety pins that are in the line of stitching as you go.

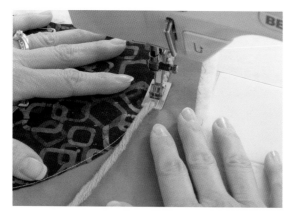

Couch yarn over seam line to cover stitching and fabric raw edge.

7. At the end of the seam line, reset the stitch length to zero and take several stitches in place to lock the thread. Trim the thread and excess yarn at the end of the seam line.

8. Continue couching over all the raw edges, removing the safety pins as you stitch.

9. When all the couching is done, remove the remaining safety pins and press the quilt from the back.

Machine Quilting

Whether you choose to couch over the raw edges or leave the raw edges to fray, machine quilting will help keep the fabric stable and help produce a thematic finish for your quilt. Overall, the quilting should be used as a design element that pulls everything together. Keep this in mind whether you're handling the machine quilting yourself or sending it off to a long-arm quilter.

When I'm doing the quilting myself, I let the quilt talk to me. Sometimes inspiration for the quilting comes to me quickly and other times I have to hang the quilt top up and wait for the ideas to come. Once I get a general idea of how to quilt an area, I often sketch out the pattern on paper to help determine how to move the quilt under the needle and also to get a general idea

Tips for Successful Couching

▮ Whenever possible, your first couched line should start at one quilt edge and run through the center width or length of the quilt. Then work from that line toward the outside edges. If there's no stitching line running completely across the quilt, start at a point near the center and work out toward the edges of the quilt.

▮ Practice couching on a sample sandwich first to check the stitch quality. This is especially true when trying a new yarn or thread for the first time. Stitch at least 3" on your sample and check the stitch on both the top and the back. If the bobbin thread is showing on the top, loosen the tension (lower the number). If the top thread is showing on the back, increase the tension (raise the number).

▮ Let the sewing machine stitch at its own pace; don't force the fabric through.

▮ If the yarn and stitching begin to bunch or tighten, increase the *length* of the zigzag stitch.

▮ If the stitching doesn't cover the yarn width, increase the width of the zigzag stitch.

▮ When you're stitching a tight turn, stop stitching with the needle down on the inside of the turn, backstitch, and then continue stitching.

of size and spacing. I like to hang the practice drawing above my sewing machine as a guide.

With the basics sketched out, I then use a chalk liner tool (these have a wheel that lays down the chalk) to block out an area where I want a specific pattern. The chalk liner lets me easily mark the quilt and stand back to preview the areas to be stitched before making the final decision on where to place my quilting. The chalk remains visible while I'm working on the quilting but is easily dusted off when I'm done.

Binding and Facing

Quilt edges in this book have been finished using one of two techniques: binding or facing. Both techniques enclose the raw edges but each presents a different look. Binding is seen on the front and back of the quilt, resulting in a frame around the quilt. A facing creates a clean finished edge by wrapping the facing strip to the back, leaving a seam on the quilt edge. This is often preferable when you have many fabric colors along the quilt edge and don't want to break up the lines.

Binding

To finish the quilt traditionally, use double-fold binding. It nicely frames the quilt.

1. Square up the quilt.

2. Cut 2"-wide straight-grain strips (selvage to selvage) from the binding fabric. You'll need enough strips to go around the quilt plus approximately 10" additional for joining strips and mitering corners.

3. With right sides together, join the strips end to end to make one long strip.

4. Trim one end of the strip at a 45° angle and press the raw angled end under ¼". This will be the beginning of the binding strip.

5. Fold the binding strip in half lengthwise, wrong sides together, and press. Your strip should now be 1" wide.

6. Starting at the middle of one edge of the layered quilt, lay the binding strip along the edge of the quilt top, raw edges aligned. Using a ¼" seam allowance, stitch the binding to the quilt, beginning several inches from the angled end. Stop sewing ¼" from the first corner; backstitch. Cut the threads and remove the quilt from the machine.

7. Rotate the quilt so you're ready to sew the next edge. Fold the binding up at a 90° angle so the fold makes a 45° angle. Fold the binding back down onto itself so the raw edges are aligned. Begin stitching at the edge, backstitch, and then continue stitching until you're ¼" from the next corner; backstitch. Repeat the folding and stitching process at each corner.

Fold the binding strip up so the fold makes a 45° angle.

Fold the binding back down onto itself, aligning the binding and quilt raw edges.

8. When you're close to the beginning of the binding, trim the end of the strip so it overlaps the beginning by approximately 1". Continue sewing the binding in place.

9. Add any desired dimensional stitching and beading.

10. Fold the binding to the back of the quilt and hand blindstitch the folded edge in place, covering the machine stitching.

Facing

Use this finishing option when you don't want to see binding fabric on the front of the finished quilt.

1. Square up the quilt.

2. Cut 4½"-wide straight-grain strips (selvage to selvage) from the facing fabric. You'll need enough strips to go around the quilt plus approximately 10" additional for joining strips and tucking corners.

3. With right sides together, join the strips end to end as needed to make four strips: two that measure the width of the quilt top plus 2", and two that measure the length of the quilt top plus 2".

4. Fold each facing strip in half lengthwise, wrong sides together, and press. The strips should now be 2¼" wide.

5. With right sides together and raw edges aligned, center and pin a facing strip to the top edge of the quilt. The facing will extend past the quilt top 1" on each side. Starting and stopping ¼" from the corners with a backstitch, stitch the facing in place.

6. Repeat step 5 with the bottom facing strip, and then press the facing's folded edge away from the quilt center.

Press facing strips away from the quilt center.

7. In the same manner, sew the side facing strips to the sides of the quilt top; press.

All of the facing strips have been attached and pressed.

8. Trim away the small triangle of excess quilt top, batting, and backing fabrics found at each corner to reduce bulk.

9. Add any desired dimensional stitching and beading.

10. Turn the top and bottom facing strips to the back so the facing doesn't show on the front, rolling the seam slightly to the back. Press from the back and then pin the facings in place. Hand blindstitch the folded edges to the backing.

11. For the side facing strips, trim the excess facing fabric at each end to ¼" from the top and bottom edges. Fold the facings to the back so the corners are tucked in and square with the top and bottom edges; press and pin in place as before. Hand blindstitch the folded edges to the backing.

By turning back the corner, you'll be able to tuck in the excess fabric and square off the corner before stitching the facing in place.

Hand Stitching

I'm a hand stitcher and love how needle and thread can be used to create line, depth, color, texture, and definition. Use it all on its own or combined with other forms of stitching finishes. In this section, I'll share my three favorite stitches that can easily transform any quilt.

Remember that you're stitching through three layers. Each time you start stitching, knot one end of the thread, and then bring the needle up from the back of the quilt at the starting point. Pull the knot gently into the batting layer to conceal it.

Running stitch. One of the most basic embroidery stitches, this stitch makes a line that can be varied easily by working stitches of different widths, lengths, and spacing. By making many rows of running stitches close together, you can create an area of texture and color.

Work a series of straight stitches from right to left. Bring the needle up through the layers and out through the quilt top at A. Insert the needle at

B, and then come out at C to begin the next stitch, sewing through all the layers.

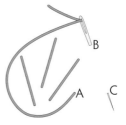

Straight stitch. This is one of the easiest and most versatile stitches, because it's made of one single stitch. Fun follows when it's worked in regular or irregular formations, varying lengths, colors, and widths.

The stitch is simple. Bring the needle up through the layers and out through the quilt top at A. Insert the needle at B, and then come out at C to begin the next stitch. Continue, sewing through all of the layers (or the top and batting only). Once you know the basic stitch, you can change its look by making stitches of irregular lengths, overlapping stitches, or using the stitch to create a variety of shapes. I've used the straight stitch to create a flower-like stitch on several quilts.

I had loads of fun using the straight stitch to create the idea of snowflakes to fill the background on "Sweet Dreams" (page 71).

Seed stitch. The seed stitch is made up of small, straight stitches of equal lengths laid perpendicular to each other. It lets you fill large areas with either light or dense covering. The stitches can be worked uniformly or randomly, and you can create many of nature's textures by using different threads and colors.

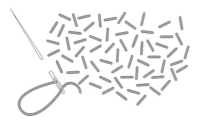

Bead Quilting

By their very nature, beads offer us the opportunity to sparkle and show off. Even more importantly, beads offer an enticing way to draw someone from across the room for a closer look at our quilts. They're an invitation to the viewer to look further, and the quilt artist's chance to entice and engage the viewer. Here you'll find instruction for my basic bead quilting by hand, where each of the beads added to the quilt is decorative while also functioning as a quilting stitch.

1. Thread the needle with a strand of strong 60-weight polyester thread and knot the ends together. Insert the needle into the top of the quilt, about 1" from where you want to place the first bead. Continue through the batting and then come out through the top of the quilt at the selected beading site.

2. Pull the knot through the quilt top and into the batting layer.

3. With the thread pulled slightly taut, take a single, tiny stitch in place through all three layers (top, batting, and backing).

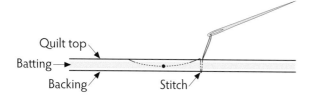

4. Pick up one bead on the needle and let it slide onto the thread.

5. With the bead on the thread, insert the needle back into the same hole the thread is emerging from and into the batting layer. Push the needle sideways through the batting and up through the quilt top at the next spot you want to add a bead. This is called traveling.

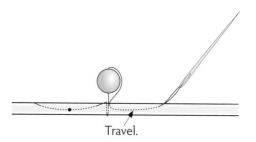

Travel.

6. Repeat steps 4 and 5 until the last bead has been added or you need to rethread your needle.

7. To finish or end your thread for rethreading, bring the threaded needle through all three layers to the back of the quilt. Take a tiny stitch through the backing only, followed by a tiny backstitch. Take another stitch over the previous stitch. Then repeat from two directions to create a small knot.

8. Bring the threaded needle through the knot and into the batting, traveling to a point about 1" from the knot. Bring the needle out through the quilt top and clip the thread. Pull the thread tail back into the batting.

2. Then bring the needle back into and out of the layers about 1" away and clip threads.

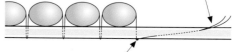

1. Stitch several times through the same stitch at the back to create a small knot.

The Projects

Simplifying, to me, applies to both design and construction, and I hope that you try out the exercises provided in "Simplify, Simplify, Simplify" on page 6. In the projects, I'll share how I used various techniques to stitch these simplified pattern designs, but there's another concept that I'm sharing with these particular projects, too: Each quilt is created in three panels rather than blocks. The panels offer a different style of construction. Additionally, they provide various finishing and hanging possibilities. So, whether you work on the panels separately or simultaneously, stitch them together into one larger quilt, or leave the panels to hang on their own or in groupings, have fun!

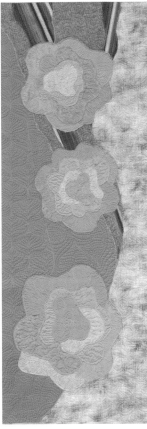

page 41

page 51

page 71

Finished panel size: 21" x 60"
Quilted by Maddie Ketray

Poppy Pods

Ruffly pom-poms—that's how the flowers of the common poppy plant are sometimes described. They are wonderful, exotically tall, somewhat top-heavy plants, and the only thing more fun than the flowers are the seedpods. The pods themselves are strange-looking things that always attract my attention while out wandering in late summer. They seem almost prehistoric in appearance, and though some may be smooth and inviting to touch, I love the funky, hairy, and even prickly examples. The pods have little top hats like whirligigs that look as if they might start spinning and take off at any moment.

For this quilt, I've simplified these fun seedpods in long, gangly designs that begged to be presented in a fantasy garden of quilting. I set each grouping of poppy pods on its own panel, but the three panels would work just as nicely as one larger quilt made from the different-height pods stitched together.

To show off the pods, I used the fused-fabric method. Then, to quilt the fantasy garden around the pods, I turned to long-arm quilt artist Maddie Ketray. The garden grew under her needle and the pods soon had a whole group of visiting plants and insects, lending the piece a level of complexity that works wonderfully with the simplicity of the pods.

Materials

In addition to the items listed in "Supplies" on page 10, you'll need the following materials. Yardage is based on 42"-wide fabric. The yardage listed for the appliqué pieces is enough for the fused-fabric backing.

Fabric	Pattern Pieces		
	Left panel	*Center panel*	*Right panel*
5¼ yards of pale-gray solid	Background	Background	Background
1¼ yards of bright-blue solid	2, 3, 5, 7, 9, 13	1, 4, 6, 7, 9, 14	1, 4, 6, 7, 9, 14
¾ yard of vivid-purple solid	11, 12, 15, 16, 17	11, 12, 15, 16, 17	11, 12, 15, 16, 17
½ yard of periwinkle-blue solid	1, 4, 6, 8, 10, 14	2, 3, 5, 8, 10, 13	2, 3, 5, 8, 10, 13
Additional Materials			
1⅞ yards of fabric for facings			
5½ yards of fabric for backing			
3 pieces, 27" x 66", of batting			
3½ yards of 17"-wide paper-backed fusible web for fused-fabric technique			

Preparing the Patterns

Refer to "Fast-Piece Appliqué Basics" on page 17.

1. Enlarge each of the panel patterns on page 35 to 22" x 61" (870% on a photocopy machine) using the desired method.

2. Use the full-sized patterns to make freezer-paper templates for each panel.

Preparing the Background and Appliqués

1. From the pale-gray solid, cut three rectangles, 22" x 61".

2. Referring to the materials list and "Fused-Fabric Elements" on page 20, use the freezer-paper templates to prepare the appliqués. Refer to "Creating Fused Appliqué Units" on page 21 to create fused appliqué units from pieces 13 and 14 and pieces 1–10 on each panel.

Assembling the Panels

Refer to "Fused-Fabric Elements" and the following instructions to construct each panel. Use the full-sized paper patterns for appliqué placement.

1. Position and tape prepared stems 12 and 16 to a background rectangle, and stitch them in place.

2. Tape prepared pieces 11 and 15 to the top of the stems, and stitch them in place.

3. Position and tape prepared poppy-pod unit 13/14 to the panel, and stitch it in place.

4. Position and tape prepared poppy-pod unit 1–10 to the panel, and stitch it in place.

5. Position, tape, and stitch prepared piece 17 in place.

Finishing

Refer to "Finishing Details" on page 25.

1. Layer each panel with batting and backing; baste the layers together.

2. Add any desired couching and machine quilting details.

3. Trim each panel to 21½" x 60½".

4. Prepare and attach facing strips to the edges of each panel, but do not hand stitch them to the backing yet. I used facing rather than binding to give the illusion of connectivity between the panels when they're hung together.

5. Add any additional hand stitching and bead quilting.

6. Fold the facings to the back of each panel and hand stitch them in place.

Display Ideas

Think of the hanging opportunities! I envision these panels hanging in the corner of a room, with two panels on one wall and the remaining panel on the adjacent wall.

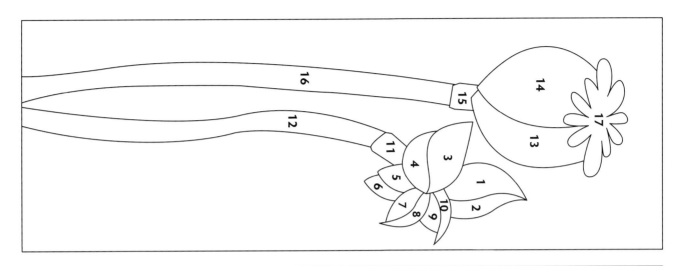

Poppy Pods
Enlarge panel 870%.
Each panel size: 21" x 60"

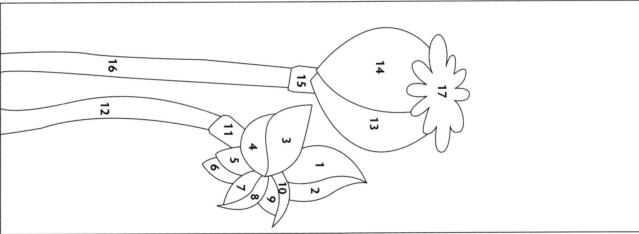

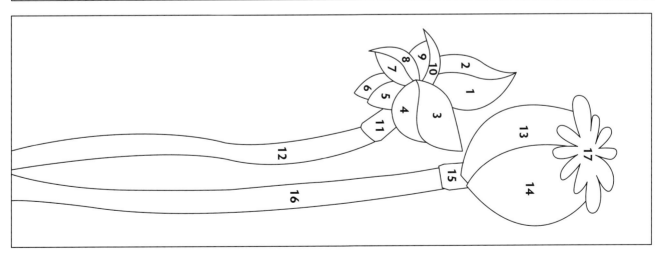

Finished panel size: 21" x 64"
Quilted by Cory Allender

Aspen Dawning

Have you ever walked among aspen trees? In spring, the color of the budding leaves always makes my heart dance. Then in summer, with even the slightest breeze, the sound of their small leaves fluttering makes me feel like I'm close to the ocean, listening to the waves. In fall, the leaves turn yellow and the glow can light up any hillside, but in winter, and really throughout the year, what I love about the aspens is their silvery white, lean, and darkly knotted trunks. These lovely trees always grow in groups known as *colonies*. These colonies are long lived, sometimes thousands of years old, nature's way of proving once again that there's benefit and safety in numbers.

Here, my own group of aspens is limited to six, but as I was designing this quilt, I couldn't help but think of how much fun it would be to have a larger grouping, one that you could walk among just like you might out in the world.

I simplified these trees by glorifying their trunks. This paring down of essentials encourages one to let the quilting speak to the details. Wanting to ensure that the trunks remained the featured elements, I used my fused-fabric method, building color and interest through the build-up of fabric to express texture and knots in the trunks.

Materials

In addition to the items listed in "Supplies" on page 10, you'll need the following materials. Yardage is based on 42"-wide fabric.

5⅝ yards of pale-green solid for background

1½ yards of beige-and-white print for tree trunks

1 yard of white-on-white print #1 for tree trunks

1 yard of white-on-white print #2 for tree trunks

1 yard of neutral stripe for bark

1 yard of light-gray solid for bark

1 yard of light-beige solid for bark

¾ yard of brown print for bark

¼ yard of black print for knots

2⅛ yards of fabric for facings

2 yards of backing fabric for fused-fabric technique

5¾ yards of fabric for backing

3 pieces, 27" x 70", of batting

3 yards of 17"-wide paper-backed fusible web for fused-fabric technique

Cutting

From the black print, cut:
2 strips, 4¼" x 42"

From the light-gray solid, cut:
2 strips, 3½" x 42"

3 strips, 3" x 42"; crosscut the strips into
   21 pieces, 3" x 6"

3 strips, 2½" x 42"; crosscut the strips into
   21 pieces, 3" x 6"

3 strips, 2" x 42"; crosscut the strips into
   21 pieces, 3" x 6"

3 strips, 1½" x 42"; crosscut the strips into
   21 pieces, 3" x 6"

3 strips, 1" x 42"; crosscut the strips into
   21 pieces, 3" x 6"

**From *each* of the neutral stripe, light-beige
solid, and brown print, cut:**
3 strips, 3" x 42"; crosscut the strips into
   21 pieces, 3" x 6" (63 total)

3 strips, 2½" x 42"; crosscut the strips into
   21 pieces, 3" x 6" (63 total)

3 strips, 2" x 42"; crosscut the strips into
   21 pieces, 3" x 6" (63 total)

3 strips, 1½" x 42"; crosscut the strips into
   21 pieces, 3" x 6" (63 total)

3 strips, 1" x 42"; crosscut the strips into
   21 pieces, 3" x 6" (63 total)

From the pale-green solid, cut:
3 rectangles, 22" x 65"

Preparing the Patterns

Refer to "Fast-Piece Appliqué Basics" on page 17.

1. Enlarge each of the panel patterns on page 40
   to 22" x 65" (995% on a photocopy machine)
   using the desired method.

2. Use the full-sized patterns to make freezer-
   paper templates for each panel. Pieces 1 and 2
   on the panels are the entire tree trunks.

Preparing the Appliqués

Refer to "Fused-Fabric Elements" on page 20.

1. Use the piece 1 and 2 freezer-paper templates
   to prepare the trunk base appliqués. Make
   the piece 1 appliqués on the left and center
   panels from the white-on-white print #1; use
   the white-on-white print #2 for piece 2 on the
   left panel and piece 1 on the right panel; and
   use the beige-and-white print for piece 2 on

the center and right panels. To make the best
use of your fabric, refer to the full-sized paper
pattern to cut the freezer-paper templates
apart crosswise at points where a knot
appliqué will cover the join.

2. To make the knot appliqués, sew a black
   4¼" x 42" strip to a light-gray 3½" x 42" strip
   to make a strip set. Repeat to make a total
   of two strip sets. Press the seam allowances
   open. Crosscut the strip sets into six
   segments, 3½" wide; five segments, 2¾" wide;
   and nine segments, 1¾" wide.

Make 2 strip sets.
Cut into segments, 3½" wide; 5 segments, 2¾" wide;
5 segments, 2½" wide; and 9 segments, 1¾" wide.

3. Referring to the photo as a guide, lay out
   the segments from step 2 and the 3" x 6"
   rectangles in groups on the full-sized paper
   pattern over the sections labeled as knots.
   The rectangles are large enough to give
   you flexibility in varying the lengths of the
   pieces used in each group, and they should be
   assembled so that they're wider and longer
   than the final appliqué. Once you're pleased
   with the selection and position of the pieces in
   each group, sew them together. Press the seam
   allowances open. Fuse each knot group to the
   backing fabric as described in "Fused-Fabric
   Elements."

4. Iron the freezer-paper template to the right
   side of the joined piece. Again, the appliqué
   will be larger than the template.

*Join a variety of rectangles and pieced segments to
make the knot appliqués.*

Assembling the Quilt Top

Refer to the following instructions to construct each panel. Use the full-sized paper patterns for appliqué placement.

1. Lay out trunk piece 1 on your work surface. Tape the knot appliqués in place on the right side of the trunk fabric. Using invisible thread, sew along the right and left edges of the freezer-paper templates, extending the stitching across the trunk width as needed.

Lay the knot groupings in place on the prepared trunk fabric, and then sew along the right and left edges of the template with invisible thread, removing the tape when you get to it.

2. Remove the templates and trim the fabric close to the stitching lines and even with the sides of the trunk fabric.

3. Repeat steps 1 and 2 for all trunks.

4. Position and tape one prepared trunk appliqué to a background rectangle. Sew the trunk in place along the long edges. Repeat with the remaining prepared trunk. Note that for the center panel, the trunk piece 1 appliqué must be stitched in place first.

Finishing

1. Layer each panel with batting and backing; baste the layers together.

2. Add any desired couching and machine quilting details.

3. Trim each panel to 21½" x 64½".

4. Prepare and attach the facing strips to the edges of each panel, but do not hand stitch them to the backing yet. I used facing rather than binding to give the illusion of connectivity between the panels when they're hung together.

5. Add any additional hand stitching or bead quilting.

6. Fold the facings to the back of each panel and hand stitch them in place.

Here you can see the shimmer and feel the fluttering movement of the leaves Cory Allender achieved in her quilting.

Display Idea

I would love to see a whole wall made up of these panels. It would certainly feel like you're walking through the aspens.

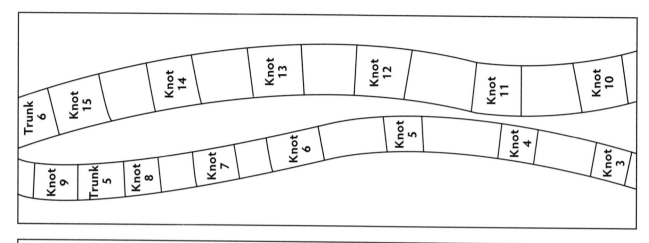

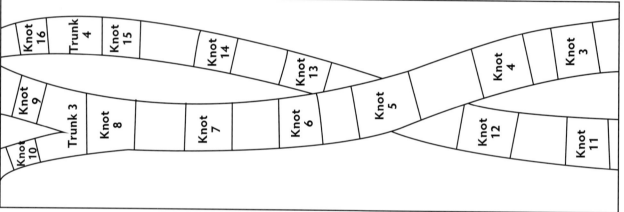

Aspen Dawning
Enlarge panel 955%.
Each panel size: 21" x 64"

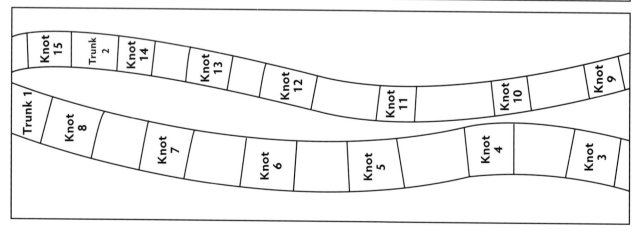

Bull's Eye Roses

During my first year living in Kentucky, I thought I had a reprieve in the garden. The original owner of my home was an avid gardener, and the professionals all say to wait a full year to see what pops up before making changes. With my travel schedule and a new home to feather and fluff, I was glad to kick back and enjoy the garden as it was. This worked for about two months, then we realized someone had thought planting ivy would be a nice addition. With ivy coming through windows, strangling the air conditioner unit, and slowly taking over, we turned to the professionals, who removed an amazing four truckloads of ivy.

This left two areas cleared and ready to fill with something fun and new. I chose Bull's Eye roses—pink with yellow centers and a lovely fragrance. In this quilt, these three panels of roses were stitched together to create a wonderful, fun, big quilt to remind me of my first big garden undertaking in my new home.

To make this quilt soft and cuddly to use on a bed or sofa, I used a variation of Fast-Piece Appliqué that doesn't use fusible web. Prewash all the fabrics, then assemble the quilt using a wash-away construction method (page 20). The quilting will hold it all together! My friend and long-arm quilter Mandy Leins came up with this method for one of her own quilt projects, and her masterful quilting turned "Bull's Eye Roses" into a treasure.

Materials

In addition to the items listed in "Supplies" on page 10, you'll need the following materials. Yardage is based on 42"- wide fabric.

Fabrics	Pattern Pieces		
Background	*Panel 1*	*Panel 2*	*Panel 3*
2 yards of summer-green solid	1B	1B	1B
2 yards of summer-green print	2B	2B	2B
1 yard of olive-green print	4B, 6B	3B, 5B	4B, 6B
1 yard of green stripe	3B, 5B	4B, 6B	3B, 5B
Roses	*Large Rose*	*Medium Rose*	*Small Rose*
1 yard of bright-pink solid	1, 8	4, 6	7, 9
1 yard of bright-pink batik	6	5, 9	1, 8
¾ yard of medium-pink solid	2, 7	3, 7	4, 6
¾ yard of medium-rose solid	3, 5	2, 8, 10	5, 10
¾ yard of pale-pink batik	4, 9	1	2, 3

Additional Materials
⅝ yard of green batik for binding
66" x 71" piece of batting
Water-soluble thread or glue (optional)

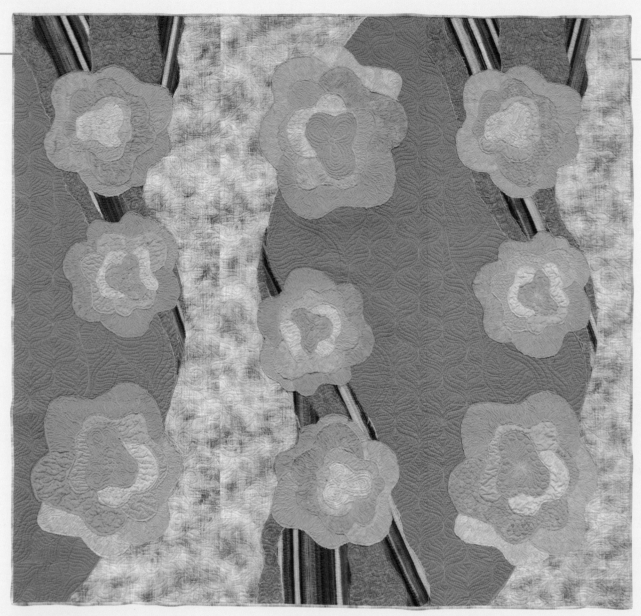

Finished quilt size: 63½" x 59½"
Quilted by Mandy Leins

Preparing the Patterns and Appliqués

Refer to "Fast-Piece Appliqué Basics" on page 17.

1. Enlarge the panel pattern on page 45 to 22" x 60" (666% on a photocopy machine) using the desired method.

2. Use the full-sized pattern to make three freezer-paper templates of each piece.

3. Referring to the materials list, use the freezer-paper templates to prepare the appliqués.

Construct the Background Panels and Appliqués

Refer to "Wash-Away Construction Variations" on page 20 for complete step-by-step instructions to use water-soluble thread or glue to construct the panels and appliqués, if desired. Pieces C–F are each one complete piece.

Background Panels

1. Using the prepared background pieces, assemble the following pairs of pieces: C and D, and E and F.

2. Join the C-D piece to the E-F piece.

3. Join piece A to the C-F unit. Add the B piece to this unit to complete the background panel.

4. Repeat steps 1–3 to make a total of three background panels.

Large Roses

1. Using the prepared large-rose pieces, assemble the following pairs of pieces: 1 and 3, 5 and 6, and 7 and 9.

2. Join the 1/3 piece to piece 4.

3. Join the 1/3/4 unit to piece 2.

4. Join the 1–4 unit to the 5/6 piece.

5. Join the 1–6 unit to piece 8.

6. Join the 1–6/8 unit to the 7/9 piece to complete a large rose.

7. Repeat steps 1–6 to make three large roses.

Medium Rose

1. Using the prepared medium-rose pieces, assemble the following pairs of pieces: 1 and 2, 4 and 5, 7 and 10, and 8 and 9.

2. Join the 1/2 piece to piece 3.

3. Join the 1–3 unit to the 4/5 piece.

4. Join the 1–5 unit to piece 6.

5. Join the 1–6 unit to the 7/10 piece.

6. Join the 1–7/10 unit to the 8/9 piece to complete a medium rose.

7. Repeat steps 1–6 to make a total of three medium roses.

Small Rose

1. Using the prepared small-rose pieces, assemble the following pairs of pieces: 1 and 2, 3 and 4, 5 and 6, 7 and 10, and 8 and 9.

2. Join the 1/2 piece to the 3/4 piece.

3. Join the 1–4 unit to the 5/6 piece.

4. Join the 1–6 unit to the 7/10 piece.

5. Join the 1–7/10 unit to the 8/9 piece to complete a small rose.

6. Repeat steps 1–5 to make three small roses.

Assembling the Quilt Top

1. Refer to "Set-On Pieces" on page 23 and the full-sized paper pattern to position and stitch one small rose, one medium rose, and one large rose on each of the three background panels.

2. Remove the freezer-paper templates and trim the outermost fabrics to the stitching line.

3. Trim each panel to 21½" x 59½". Sew the panels together along the long edges, rotating the center panel to add variety to the overall design. Refer to the photo on page 42.

Finishing

Refer to "Finishing Details" on page 25.

1. Layer the quilt top with batting and backing; baste the layers together.

2. Add any desired couching and machine quilting details.

3. Prepare and attach the binding, but do not fold it to the back.

4. Add any additional hand stitching and bead quilting.

5. Fold the binding to the back of the quilt and hand stitch it in place.

Display Idea

Spread this quilt across your bed and enjoy the feeling of napping in the garden.

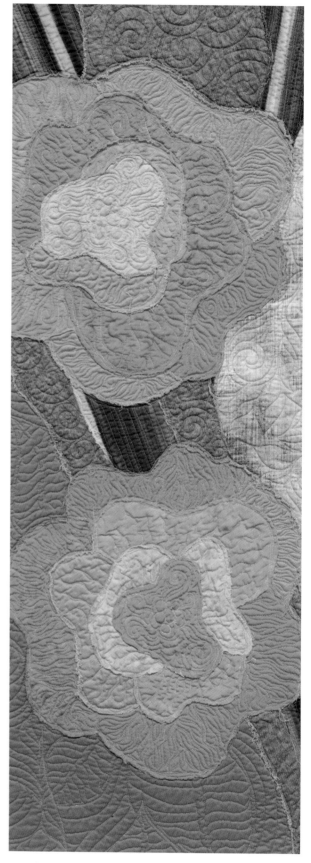

Fun frayed edges are produced when a wash-away construction method is used.

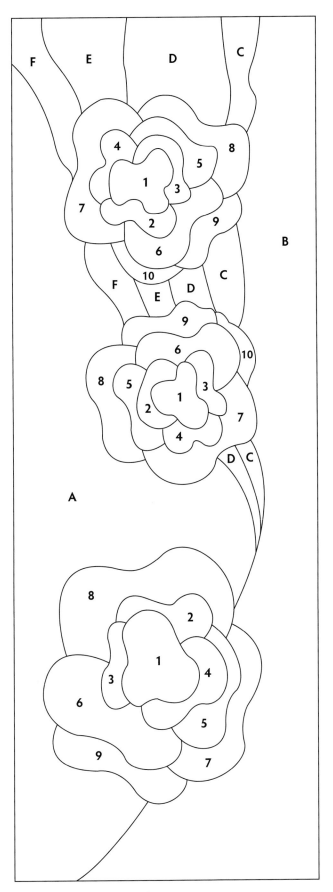

Bull's Eye Roses
Enlarge panel 666%.
Panel size: 22" x 60"

Finished quilt size: 59½" x 72½"
Quilted by Lisa Sipes

Umbrella Beach

Have you ever been to a beach where the water was so blue and inviting that you never wanted to leave? Luckily for me, as I walked along such a beach in the Caribbean, I spied umbrellas all lined up, waiting to provide a little shade, making it possible to linger and enjoy it all.

I'm sure the locals had a name for this patch of sand along the boardwalk, but to me it will always be Umbrella Beach. In reality, this scene needed little simplifying. The bright oranges and reds of the umbrellas along with the sand, surf, and sky were all one could see or want to remember.

This quilt starts with one enlarged pattern which is cut apart on two of the curved lines to make individual panels. Once the panels are made, they're sewn back together. The umbrellas in each panel remain very similar, but the background called for more subtle differences, requiring the same from my pattern.

Because I wanted this quilt to be quilted on a long-arm machine, I used Fast-Piece Appliqué stitched with invisible thread. I also wanted the quilting to provide a strong idea of sand, water, and sky. That's where long-arm quilter Lisa Sipes stepped in. Her quilting design unified the panels with her treatment of the sky and ocean as one, just as it seemed while walking along the beach in St. Martin.

Materials

In addition to the items listed in "Supplies" on page 10, you'll need the following materials. Yardage is based on 42"-wide fabric.

Fabric	Pattern Pieces		
	Top panel	*Center panel*	*Bottom panel*
2 yards of bright-blue mottled print	3, 5, 6, 7	6, 7, 8	4, 5, 9, 10, 11
1½ yards of light-blue batik	1	1	1
2 yards of light-tan batik	4, 8, 9	—	6, 7, 8
1½ yards of beige batik	2	2, 3, 4, 5	2, 3
1 yard of red-orange-and-yellow mottled print	15, 17, 21, 24, 25	14, 16, 18, 21, 23	16, 18, 23, 25, 27
½ yard of red-on-red dot	14, 16	13, 15, 17	22, 24, 26
½ yard of orange-on-orange dot	20, 22, 23	22, 24	17, 19
1 fat quarter (18" x 21") of reddish-orange solid	13, 19	12, 20	15, 20
1 fat quarter of brown solid	10, 11, 12, 18	9, 10, 11, 19	12, 13, 14, 21

Additional Materials

⅝ yard of orange fabric for binding

3⅝ yards of fabric for backing

65" x 78" piece of batting

Preparing the Patterns and Appliqués

Refer to "Fast-Piece Appliqué Basics" on page 17.

1. Enlarge the pattern on page 49 to 60" x 73" (1000% on a photocopy machine) using the desired method.

2. Cut apart the pattern along the dashed lines to make three separate patterns.

3. Use the full-sized patterns to make freezer-paper templates for each panel.

4. Referring to the materials list, use the freezer-paper templates to prepare the appliqués.

Construct the Panels

Refer to "Fast-Piece Appliqué Basics" for complete step-by-step instructions to construct each panel.

Top Panel

1. Using the templates for the top panel, assemble the following pairs of pieces: 1 and 2, 3 and 4, 5 and 8, 6 and 9, 12 and 13, 14 and 15, 16 and 17, 18 and 19, 20 and 25, 21 and 23, and 22 and 24.

2. Join the 1/2 piece to the 3/4 piece, the 21/23 piece to the 22/24 piece, and the 14/15 piece to the 16/17 piece.

3. Join the 1–4 unit to the 12/13 piece, the 5/8 piece to piece 10, the 6/9 piece to piece 11, and the 20/21/23/25 unit to the 22/24 piece.

4. Join the 1–4/12/13 unit to the 18/19 piece. Add piece 7 to this unit.

5. Join the 6/9/11 unit to the 20–25 unit.

6. Join the 14–17 unit to the 5/8/10 unit.

7. Join the 1–4/7/12/13/18/19 unit to the 6/9/11/20–25 unit.

8. Join the 5/8/10/14–17 unit to the 1–4/6/7/9/11–13/18–25 unit to complete the panel.

Center Panel

1. Using the templates for the center panel, assemble the following pairs of pieces: 2 and 11, 3 and 19, 4 and 7, 5 and 8, 6 and 9, 13 and 16, 14 and 17, 15 and 18, 21 and 22, and 23 and 24.

2. Join the 2/11 piece to the 3/19 piece, the 4/7 piece to piece 10, the 13/16 piece to the 14/17 piece, and the 21/22 piece to the 23/24 piece.

3. Join the 4/7/10 unit to the 5/8 piece, the 13/14/16/17 unit to piece 12, and piece 20 to the 21–24 unit.

4. Join the 4/5/7/8/10 unit to the 20–24 unit.

5. Join the 12/13/14/16/17 unit to the 15/18 piece.

6. Join the 2/3/11/19 unit to the 6/9 piece.

7. Join the 2/3/6/9/11/19 unit to the 12–18 unit.

8. Join the 2/3/6/9/11–19 unit to the 4/5/7/8/10/20–24 unit. Add piece 1 to this unit to complete the panel.

Bottom Panel

1. Using the templates for the bottom panel, assemble the following pairs of pieces: 1 and 2, 3 and 5, 4 and 6, 7 and 11, 8 and 10, 14 and 15, 16 and 17, 18 and 19, 22 and 25, 23 and 26, and 24 and 27.

2. Join the 1/2 piece to the 4/6 piece, the 7/11 piece to piece 21, the 8/10 piece to piece 13, the 16/17 piece to the 18/19 piece, and the 22/25 piece to the 23/26 piece.

3. Join the 1/2/4/6 unit to piece 9, the 18/19 piece to piece 20, the 22/23/25/26 unit to the 24/27 piece, and the 14/15 piece to the 16–20 unit.

4. Join the 1/2/4/6/9 unit to piece 12, the 8/10/13 unit to the 22–27 unit, and the 7/11/21 unit to the 3/5 piece.

5. Join the 3/5/7/11/21 unit to the 8/10/13/22–27 unit.

6. Join the 3/5/7/8/10/11/13/21–27 unit to the 14–20 unit.

7. Join the 3/5/7/8/10/11/13–27 unit to the 1/2/4/6/9/12 unit to complete the panel.

Assemble the Quilt Top

1. Refer to the full-sized pattern to join the top, center, and bottom panels.

2. Remove the freezer-paper templates.

3. Trim the quilt to 59½" x 72½".

Finishing

Refer to "Finishing Details" on page 25.

1. Layer the quilt top with batting and backing; baste the layers together.

2. Add any desired couching and machine quilting details.

3. Prepare and attach the binding but do not fold it to the back.

4. Add any additional hand stitching and bead quilting.

5. Fold the binding to the back of the quilt and hand stitch it in place.

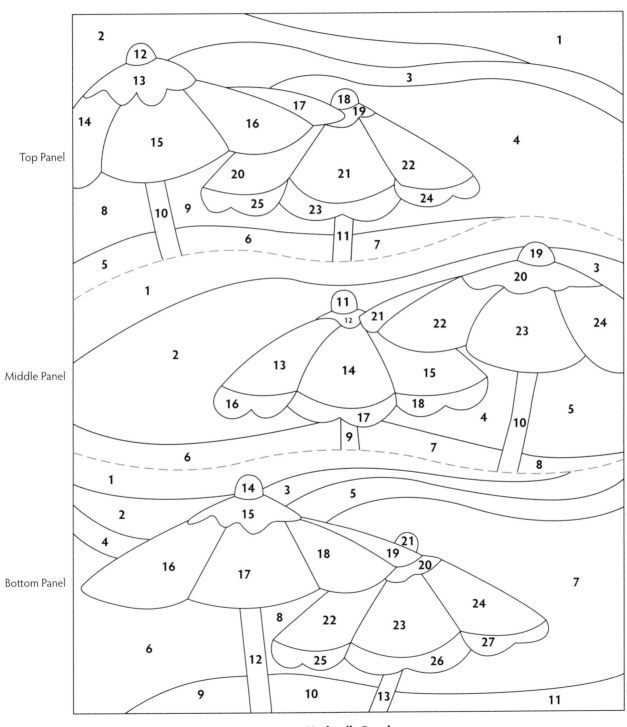

Umbrella Beach
Enlarge panel 1000%.
Panel size: 60" x 73"

Finished quilt size: 60½" x 72½"
Quilted by Vicki Tymczyszyn

Fields Full of Posies

Wildflowers are my absolute favorite part of spring and summer. I love seeing fields and hillsides covered in flowers. These colorful little gems can warm the heart, and they inspired this large quilt, bright with pink flowers on a warm, sunny day.

I used Fast-Piece Appliqué to make the large, simple flowers first, and then set them in place on the panel backgrounds. Wanting to use couching around the flowers, I sent this quilt off to long-arm quilter Vicki Tymczyszyn, asking her to echo quilt around the flowers themselves. This left me room to apply the couching details *after* the quilt was returned.

Materials

In addition to the items listed in "Supplies" on page 10, you'll need the following materials. Yardage is based on 42"-wide fabric. You'll be making multiples of pieces 1–7. Refer to the list below for the total number of pieces and to the pattern for the exact shapes, because some shapes with the same number vary slightly.

Fabric	Pattern Pieces		
	Left panel	*Center panel*	*Right panel*
3½ yards of pale-yellow tone on tone	Background	—	Background
1¾ yards of coordinating pale yellow-on-white print	—	Background	—
1 yard of pink batik #1	1 *each* of pieces 3, 4, 5, 6, 7	2 *each* of pieces 3, 4, 5, 6, 7	2 *each* of pieces 3, 4, 5, 6, 7
1 yard of pink batik #2	2 *each* of pieces 3, 4, 5, 6, 7	1 *each* of pieces 3, 4, 5, 6, 7	1 *each* of pieces 3, 4, 5, 6, 7
½ yard of green solid	3 of piece 1	3 of piece 1	3 of piece 1
1 fat quarter (18" x 21") of golden yellow	3 of piece 2	3 of piece 2	3 of piece 2
Additional Materials			
⅔ yard of yellow fabric for binding			
3½ yards of fabric for backing			
68" x 80" piece of batting			

Preparing the Patterns

Refer to "Fast-Piece Appliqué Basics" on page 17.

1. Enlarge each of the panel patterns on page 53 to 25" x 61" (870% on a photocopy machine) using the desired method.

2. Use the full-sized patterns to make freezer-paper templates for each panel.

Preparing the Backgrounds and Appliqués

1. From the pale yellow tone on tone, cut two rectangles, 25" x 61", for the background of the right and left panels.

2. From the yellow-on-white print, cut one rectangle, 25" x 61", for the background of the center panel.

3. Referring to the materials list and "Fast-Piece Appliqué Basics," use the freezer-paper templates to prepare the appliqués, making the petals for five flowers from pink batik #1 and the petals for four flowers from pink batik #2.

Constructing the Appliqués

Refer to "Fast-Piece Appliqué Basics" for complete step-by-step instructions to construct each panel. Use the full-sized pattern for appliqué placement.

1. Using the templates for one flower cut from the same fabric, assemble the following pairs of pieces: 1 and 3; and 2 and 7.

2. Join the 2/7 piece to piece 4.

3. Join the 2/4/7 unit to piece 5.

4. Join the 2/4/5/7 unit to piece 6.

5. Join the 2/4–6 unit to the 1/3 piece to complete the flower.

6. Repeat steps 1–5 to make a total of nine flowers.

Assembling the Quilt Top

1. Referring to "Set-On Pieces" on page 23, position and tape three flower appliqués to each background rectangle, and stitch them in place.

2. Remove the freezer-paper templates and trim the outermost fabrics to the stitching line.

3. Trim each panel to 24½" x 60½". Sew the panels together along the long edges.

Finishing

Refer to "Finishing Details" on page 25.

1. Layer the quilt top with batting and backing; baste the layers together.

2. Add any desired couching and machine quilting details.

3. Prepare and attach the binding but do not fold it to the back.

4. Add any additional hand stitching and bead quilting.

5. Fold the binding to the back of the quilt and hand stitch it in place.

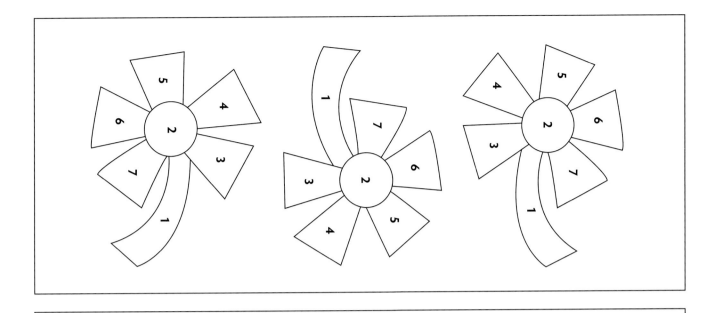

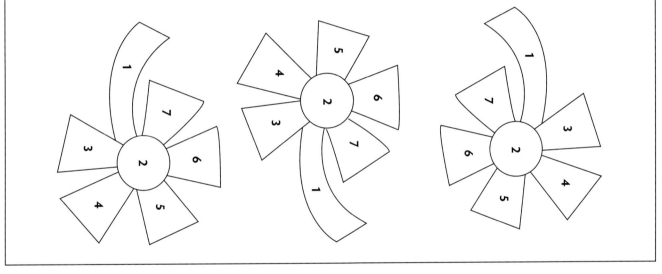

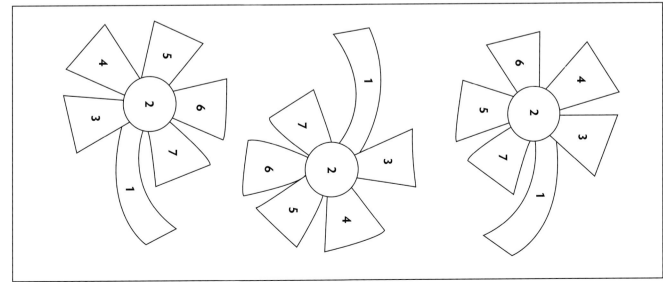

Finished panel size: 21" x 55"
Quilted by Angela Walters

Fan Faire

During the summer of 2013, I gave my blog readers a five-minute summer word design challenge—a list of words for every day between the summer solstice and fall equinox. These words worked their way into several quilt designs, and this project is an example of one of the designs I came up with for the word *fan.*

These long, lean flowers look like fans and are all the same pattern placed at different heights in order to provide depth and interest. I wanted the fans to dominate the design while giving ample opportunity for the quilting to take an active role, so I used my fused-fabric method because it allowed me to build up the fans as the featured design element in each panel.

You never know where or when your next design may come to you. You may even want to come up with your own list of words and give yourself five minutes, a pencil, and a piece of paper, and see what happens! For my list of summer words, go to my blog at http://RoseHughes.blogspot.com/2013/06/summer -words-for-sources.html.

Materials

In addition to the items listed in "Supplies" on page 10, you'll need the following materials. Yardage is based on 42"-wide fabric. The yardage listed for the appliqué pieces is enough for the fused-fabric backing.

Fabric	Pattern Pieces		
	Left panel	*Center panel*	*Right panel*
2 yards of bright-apple-green solid	Background, 4	2	Background, 4
2 yards of bright-fuchsia solid	1, 3	Background, 4	1, 3
1½ yards of bright-orange solid	2	1, 3	2
Additional Materials			
1⅞ yards of fabric for facings			
5⅛ yards of fabric for backings			
3 pieces, 27" x 61", of batting			
5 yards of 17"-wide paper-backed fusible web for fused-fabric technique			

Preparing the Patterns

Refer to "Fast-Piece Appliqué Basics" on page 17.

1. Enlarge each of the panel patterns on page 57 to 22" x 56" (835% on a photocopy machine) using the desired method.

2. Use the full-sized patterns to make freezer-paper templates for each panel.

Preparing the Backgrounds and Appliqués

1. From the green solid, cut two rectangles, 22" x 56".

2. From the fuchsia solid, cut one rectangle, 22" x 56".

3. Referring to the materials list and "Fused-Fabric Elements" on page 20, use the freezer-paper templates to prepare each appliqué.

Assembling the Panels

Refer to "Set-On Pieces" on page 23 to construct each panel, and to the photo on page 54 for the correct color pieces for each panel. Use the full-sized patterns for appliqué placement.

1. Position and tape piece 4 on piece 3, and stitch it in place.

2. Position and tape unit 3/4 on piece 2, and stitch it in place.

3. Position and tape piece 1 to the background fabric, and stitch it in place.

4. Center the 2/3/4 unit inside the opening of piece 1; tape, and then stitch it in place.

Finishing

Refer to "Finishing Details" on page 25.

1. Layer each panel with batting and backing; baste the layers together.

2. Add any desired couching and machine quilting details.

3. Trim each panel to 21½" x 55½".

4. Prepare and attach facing strips to the edges of each panel, but do not hand stitch them to the backing yet. I used facing rather than binding to give the illusion of connectivity between the panels when they're hung together.

5. Add any additional hand stitching or bead quilting.

6. Fold the facings to the back of each panel and hand stitch them in place.

Angela Walters added her quilting magic to each of the panels. Would you believe the idea for these quilted panels came from a box fan?

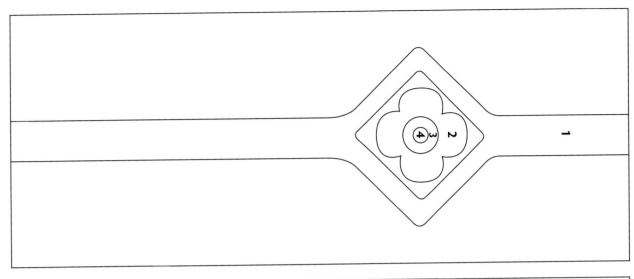

Fan Faire
Enlarge panel 835%.
Each panel size: 22" x 56"

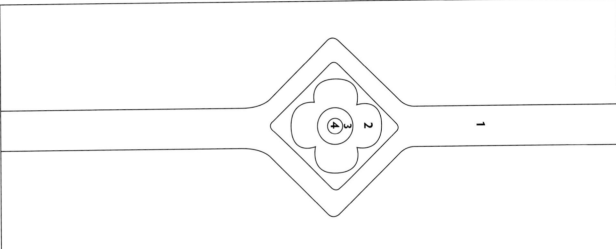

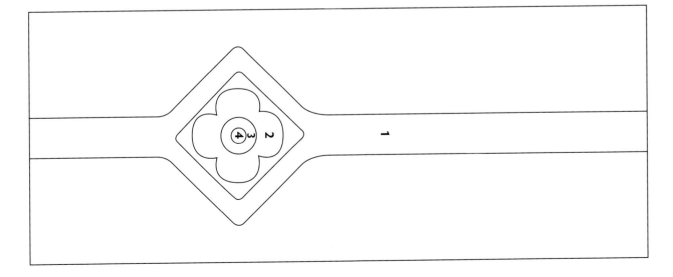

Finished quilt size: 60½" x 42"

Seedpod Polka

Seedpods have always intrigued me, and I know my husband thinks I'm crazy when I bring home especially funky-looking examples. Seedpods can make an appearance almost anytime during the year, but in late summer, a walk through open fields, wooded trails, or around ponds will surely turn up some great specimens. For inspiration, I find that the stranger they are, the better. If you can't wait until nature supplies the perfect example, an Internet search may turn up some great samples to inspire you, too. Begin your search for images of hibiscus, day lilies, or the very popular lotus seedpods. You won't be disappointed.

My seedpod designs for this quilt were simplified and stylized during a drawing session with my art group. Each of us found and brought in examples of seedpods and leaves that were soon transformed into designs for many future projects.

The seedpods for this quilt were created separately using Fast-Piece Appliqué stitching methods with clear thread. Then I stitched them in place on the panels using the set-on method.

Materials

In addition to the items listed in "Supplies" on page 10, you'll need the following materials. Yardage is based on 42"-wide fabric.

Fabric	Pattern Pieces		
	Left panel	*Center panel*	*Right panel*
1 yard of light-apple-green solid	Background	Background	Background
1 yard of light-apple-green batik	Background	Background	Background
¾ yard of red-and-orange batik	3, 5	9	3, 5
½ yard of black batik	1, 7	6	1, 7
½ yard of gold solid	4, 8, 10, 12, 14, 16, 18, 20	1, 5	4, 8, 10, 12, 14, 16, 18, 20
¼ yard of purple-and-red batik	9, 11, 13, 15, 17, 19, 21	3, 7	9, 11, 13, 15, 17, 19, 21
¼ yard of orange print	—	4	—
¼ yard of medium-green solid	—	2, 8	—
1 fat quarter (18" x 21") of mint-green solid	2, 6		2, 6
Additional Materials			
½ yard of fabric for binding			
2¾ yards of fabric for backing			
48" x 66" piece of batting			

Preparing the Patterns

Refer to "Fast-Piece Appliqué Basics" on page 17.

1. Enlarge each of the panel patterns on page 61 to 21" x 42" (660% on a photocopy machine) using the desired method.

2. Use the full-sized patterns to make freezer-paper templates for each panel, treating pieces 8–21 of the left and right panels as one piece.

3. Using the full-sized pattern for the left panel, refer to "Paper Piecing" on page 23 to trace the unit with pieces 8–21 onto foundation paper, including all of the lines and numbers. Repeat with the right panel.

Preparing the Backgrounds

1. From each of the green-solid and green-batik, cut three strips, 11" x 42".

2. Sew each green solid strip to a green batik strip along the long edges. Press the seam allowances open.

Preparing the Appliqués

Refer to "Fast-Piece Appliqué Basics" for complete step-by-step instructions to construct each panel.

Left and Right Panels

1. Referring to "Paper Piecing" and using the foundation pattern you traced earlier, paper piece sections 8–21 of the left and right panels, alternating the gold solid and purple-and-red fabrics as indicated in the materials list. Referring to "Fast-Piece Appliqué Basics," use the pieced fabric and the combined section 8–21 freezer-paper pattern to make the appliqués.

2. Referring to the materials list and "Fast-Piece Appliqué Basics," use the remaining freezer-paper templates for the right and left panels to prepare the remaining appliqués.

3. Using the appliqués for the left panel, assemble the following pairs of pieces: 1 and 2, 3 and 4, and 5 and 6.

4. Join piece 7 to the paper-pieced unit.

5. Join the 1/2 piece to the 3/4 piece to complete the head section.

6. Join the 5/6 piece to the 7–21 unit to complete the body section.

7. Repeat steps 3–6 with the appliqués for the right panel.

Center Panel

1. Referring to the materials list and "Fast-Piece Appliqué Basics," use the freezer-paper templates for the center panel to prepare the appliqués.

2. Assemble the following pairs of pieces: 1 and 2, 4 and 5, and 7 and 8.

3. Join the 1/2 piece to piece 3 to complete the head section.

4. Join the 4/5 piece to piece 6.

5. Join the 7/8 piece to piece 9.

6. Join the 4–6 unit to the 7–9 unit to complete the body section.

Assembling the Quilt Top

1. Refer to "Set-On Pieces" on page 23 and the full-sized paper patterns to position and stitch the appliqués to their appropriate panels, paying careful attention to the position of the green background fabrics.

2. Remove the freezer-paper templates and trim the outermost fabrics to the stitching line.

3. Trim each panel to 20½" x 42". Sew the panels together along the long edges.

Finishing

Refer to "Finishing Details" on page 25.

1. Layer the quilt top with batting and backing; baste the layers together.

2. Add any desired couching and machine quilting details.

3. Prepare and attach the binding but do not fold it to the back.

4. Add any additional hand stitching and bead quilting.

5. Fold the binding to the back of the quilt and hand stitch it in place.

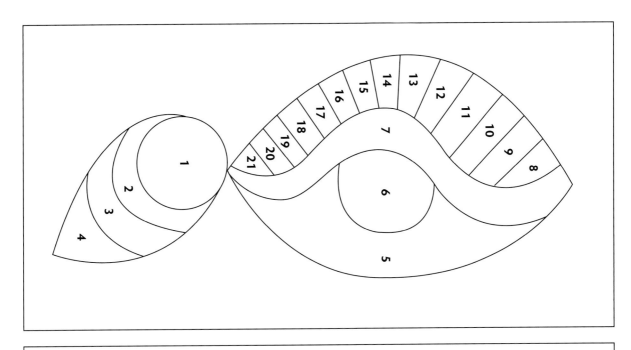

Seedpod Polka
Enlarge panel 660%.
Each panel size: 21" x 42"

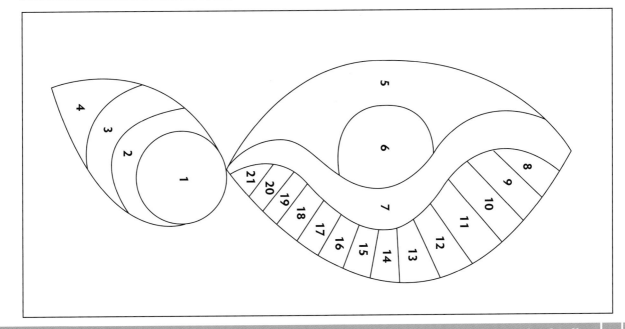

Finished panel size: 20" x 42"

Fast-Piece Appliqué

Gone Fruity for Meadow Orchards

This past summer, my husband and I traveled the back roads to all sorts of new-to-us destinations. We had a blast, but the best part was traveling the roads themselves—going over rolling hills and through farmland scattered with barns, horses, and fruit trees. I designed this quilt to serve as a reminder of all those long drives and all our future meadow orchard finds.

The numerous colors, textures, and line changes were important elements of this design, so I used Fast-Piece Appliqué to construct the three-panel landscape. It's the perfect method when you want to use a wider variety of fabrics that open up finishing-design opportunities.

Materials

In addition to the items listed in "Supplies" on page 10, you'll need the following materials. Yardage is based on 42"-wide fabric.

Fabric	Pattern Pieces		
	Left panel	*Center panel*	*Right panel*
1 yard of light-blue solid	1	1	1
1 yard of bright-fuchsia print	6, 8, 9	10, 11, 18, 19, 20	6, 8, 9
1 yard of apple-green solid	7	17	7
¾ yard of green solid	11	4, 27	11
¾ yard of light-green solid	5*, 10	3, 12	5*, 10
½ yard of gold solid	18, 19, 20, 21, 22, 24, 25, 26, 27, 28	22, 23, 24, 25, 26	18, 19, 20, 21, 22, 24, 25, 26, 27, 28
1 fat quarter (18" x 21") of medium-blue solid	2*	2*	2*
1 fat eighth (9" x 21") of brown solid	4	14*	4
1 fat eighth of blue-green-and-orange striped batik**	3	—	3
1 fat eighth of red solid	12, 13, 14, 15, 16, 17, 23	21	12, 13, 14, 15, 16, 17, 23
1 fat eighth of orange solid	—	5, 6, 7, 8, 9, 13, 15, 16	—

Additional Materials

1⅔ yards of fabric for facings
4 yards of fabric for backing
3 pieces, 26" x 48", of batting

*Set-in pieces
**The roof fabric was pieced together from two solid fabrics to create a striped fabric.

Preparing the Patterns and Appliqués

Refer to "Fast-Piece Appliqué Basics" on page 17.

1. Enlarge each of the panel patterns on page 65 to 21" x 43" (660% on a photocopy machine) using the desired method.

2. Use the full-sized patterns to make freezer-paper templates for each panel.

3. Referring to the materials list, use the freezer-paper templates to prepare the appliqués, noting that the pieces in the materials list with an asterisk will be set into other pieces and should be prepared following the instructions for "Set-In Pieces" on page 22.

Assembling the Panels

Refer to "Fast-Piece Appliqué Basics," "Set-In Pieces," "Set-On Pieces" (page 23), and the following instructions to construct each panel. Use the full-sized paper patterns for appliqué placement.

Left and Right Panels

1. Using the appliqués for the left panel, set piece 2 into piece 1, and piece 5 into piece 4.

2. Join piece 3 to the 4/5 unit.

3. Set the 3–5 unit into the 1/2 unit.

4. Join piece 6 to piece 7.

5. Set pieces 12–16 onto piece 11. Join this unit to piece 10.

6. Join the 10–16 unit to piece 8.

7. Join the 8/10–16 unit to piece 9.

8. Join pieces 18–22 to piece 17, one at a time. Join pieces 24–28 to piece 23, one at a time.

9. Set the 17–22 unit and the 23–28 unit into the 6/7 piece. Join this unit to the 8–16 unit.

10. Join the 1–5 unit to the 6–28 unit to complete the panel.

11. Remove the freezer-paper templates and trim the outermost fabrics to the stitching line.

12. Repeat steps 1–11, using the appliqués for the right panel.

Center Panel

1. Using the appliqués for the middle panel, set piece 2 into piece 1, and piece 14 into piece 27.

2. Set pieces 5–9 onto piece 4. Join this unit to piece 3.

3. Join the 3–9 unit to piece 11.

4. Set pieces 13, 15, and 16 onto the 14/27 unit. Join this unit to piece 12.

5. Join the 12–16/27 unit to piece 10. Join this unit to piece 18.

6. Join pieces 22–26 to piece 21, one at a time.

7. Join piece 20 to piece 17.

8. Join the 17/20 unit to piece 19. Set the 21–26 unit into this unit.

9. Join the 1–9/11 piece to the 10/12–16/18/27 unit.

10. Join the 1–12/16/18/27 unit to the 17/19–26 unit to complete the panel.

11. Remove the freezer-paper templates and trim the outermost fabrics to the stitching line.

Finishing

Refer to "Finishing Details" on page 25.

1. Layer each panel with batting and backing; baste the layers together.

2. Add any desired couching and machine quilting details.

3. Trim each panel to 20½" x 42½".

4. Prepare and attach facing strips to the edges of each panel, but do not hand stitch them to the backing yet. I used facing rather than binding to give the illusion of connectivity between the panels when they're hung together.

5. Add any additional hand stitching and bead quilting.

6. Fold the facings to the back of each panel and hand stitch them in place.

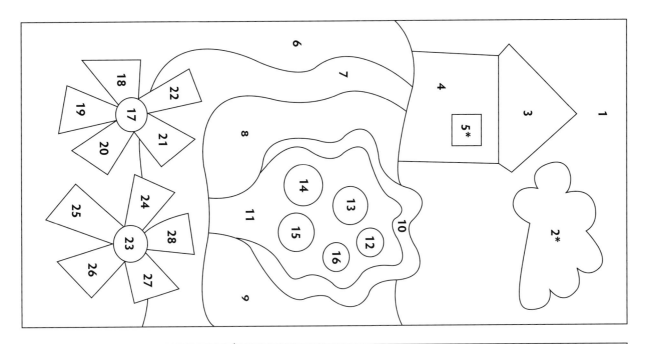

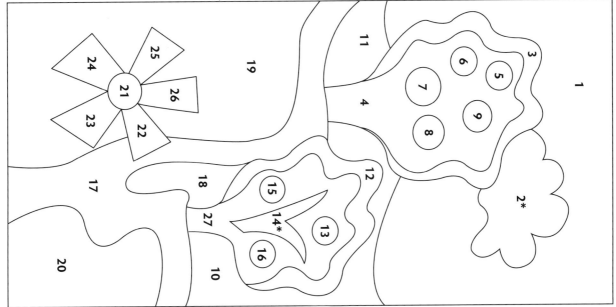

Gone Fruity For Meadow Orchards
Enlarge panel 660%.
Each panel size: 21" x 43"
*Set-in pieces

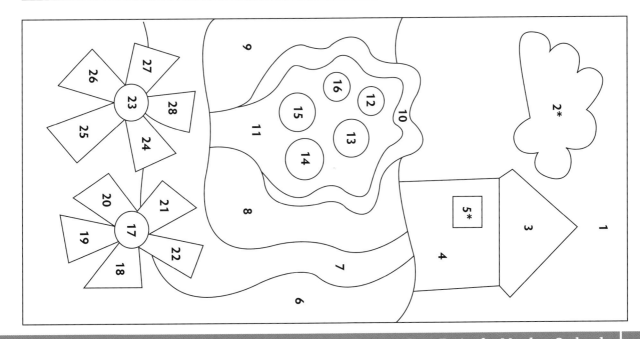

Finished panel size: 22" x 50"

Fast-Piece Appliqué

Sun's Up

The rolling hills of northern California are beautiful and inviting. There are well-worn pathways winding through the tall redwoods, leading you into the mountains or down to the rugged beaches. Early on a clear day, the sun slowly spreads light and color to these hills, permanently leaving an imprint on anyone that is lucky enough to see them.

This quilt design simplifies each element of this experience. Simple hills with simple pathways, and all the while the trees are reaching to the sky in the same way as their real-life models, though each is very simply portrayed.

Design simplicity is carried through with the color and textures of the fabrics chosen, and because I knew I wanted to use couching throughout, I used Fast-Piece Appliqué to construct these three panels.

Materials

In addition to the items listed in "Supplies" on page 10, you'll need the following materials. Yardage is based on 42"-wide fabric.

Fabric	Pattern Pieces		
	Left panel	*Center panel*	*Right panel*
3 yards of medium-blue solid	1	1	1
2 yards of purple mottled print	15, 17	10	12, 14
1 yard of yellow solid	16	19	13
1 fat quarter (18" x 21") of solid yellow silk	2*	—	—
1 fat quarter of reddish-brown solid	14	12, 15	2
1 fat quarter of red solid	13	11, 16	3
1 fat quarter of multicolored stripe**	11, 12	13, 14, 17, 18	4, 5

Additional Materials

1⅔ yards of fabric for facings
4⅞ yards of fabric for backings
3 pieces, 28" x 58", of batting

*Set-in piece
**The house fabric was pieced together from several different-colored solid fabrics to create a striped fabric.

Preparing the Patterns

Refer to "Fast-Piece Appliqué Basics" on page 17.

1. Enlarge each of the panel patterns on page 69 to 23" x 51" (775% on a photocopy machine) using the desired method.

2. Use the full-sized patterns to make freezer-paper templates for each panel, noting that piece 2 of the left panel will be set into piece 1 and should be prepared following the instructions for "Set-In Pieces" on page 22.

Assembling the Panels

Refer to "Fast-Piece Appliqué Basics," "Set-In Pieces," "Set-On Pieces" (page 23), and the following instructions to construct each panel. Use the full-sized paper patterns for appliqué placement.

Left Panel

1. Using the templates for the left panel, assemble the following pairs of pieces: 3 and 4, 6 and 7, 9 and 10, 11 and 12, 13 and 14, and 15 and 16.

2. Join the 3/4 piece to piece 5 and the 6/7 piece to piece 8.

3. Join the 3–5 unit to the 6–8 unit. Join this unit to the 9/10 piece.

4. Join the 11/12 piece to the 13/14 piece.

5. Join the 15/16 piece to piece 17.

6. Set piece 2 into piece 1.

7. Set the 3–10 unit and the 11–14 unit into the 1/2 unit.

8. Join the 1–14 unit to the 15–17 unit to complete the panel.

9. Remove the freezer-paper templates and trim the outermost fabrics to the stitching line.

Center Panel

1. Using the templates for the center panel, assemble the following pairs of pieces: 2 and 3, 4 and 5, 6 and 7, 8 and 9, 11 and 12, 13 and 14, 15 and 16, and 17 and 18.

2. Join the 11/12 piece to the 13/14 piece and the 15/16 piece to the 17/18 piece.

3. Set the 2/3, 4/5, 6/7, and 8/9 pieces onto piece 1 one at a time.

4. Set the 11–14 and 15–18 units onto piece 10 one at a time.

5. Set piece 19 onto piece 10.

6. Join the 1–9 unit to the 10–19 unit to complete the panel.

7. Trim the outermost fabrics to the stitching line.

Right Panel

1. Using the templates for the right panel, assemble the following pairs of pieces: 2 and 3, 4 and 5, 6 and 7, 8 and 9, 10 and 11, and 12 and 13.

2. Join the 2/3 piece to the 4/5 piece.

3. Join the 12/13 piece to piece 14.

4. Set the 2–5 unit into piece 1.

5. Set the 6/7, 8/9, and 10/11 pieces into piece 1 one at a time.

6. Join the 1–11 unit to the 12–14 unit to complete the panel.

7. Remove the freezer-paper templates and trim the outermost fabrics to the stitching line.

Finishing

Refer to "Finishing Details" on page 25.

1. Layer each panel with batting and backing; baste the layers together.

2. Add any desired couching and machine quilting details.

3. Trim each panel to 22½" x 50½".

4. Prepare and attach facing strips to the edges of each panel, but do not hand stitch them to the backing yet. I used facing rather than binding to give the illusion of connectivity between the panels when they're hung together.

5. Add any additional hand stitching and bead quilting.

6. Fold the facings to the back of each panel and hand stitch them in place.

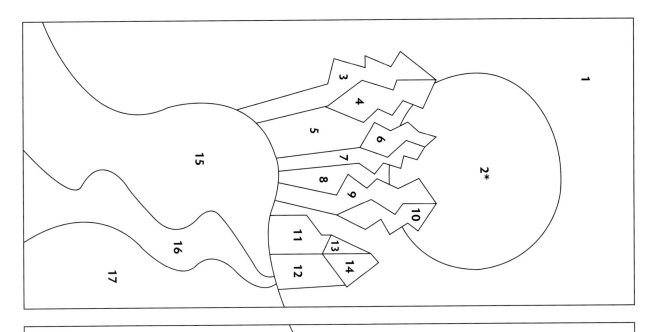

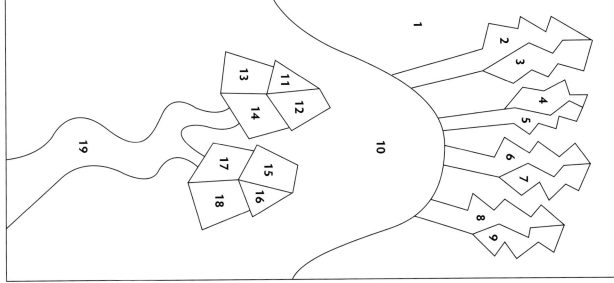

Sun's Up
Enlarge panel 755%.
Each panel size: 23" x 51"
*Set-in piece

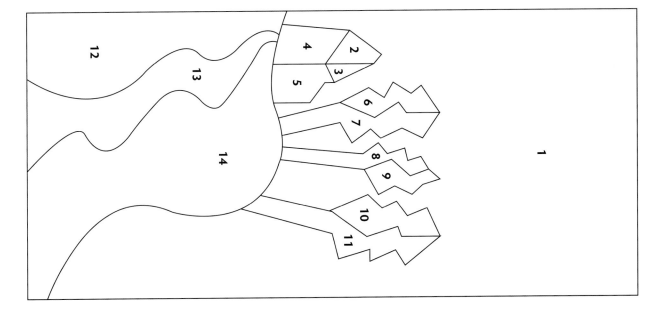

Finished panel size: 18" x 39"

Sweet Dreams

A walk through a park on a cool morning during the winter holiday season is a special time. It may require extra bundling up, and having a warm shoulder to lean on can make it extra special, but it's the light of a new day beginning that makes it all worthwhile. It all seems magical—you only need to close your eyes for a minute to imagine stars and ornaments popping into the scene. I hope you're inspired by this simplified yet inviting celebration of winter.

Look closely at the three panels for this quilt and you'll notice that the outer panel on the left is reversed to create the pattern for the panel on the right. The center has its own pattern, and while the designs on these panels are simple and may be accomplished by various appliqué methods, I selected Fast-Piece Appliqué because it allowed me to use several fabrics and open up the design opportunities.

Materials

In addition to the items listed in "Supplies" on page 10, you'll need the following materials. Yardage is based on 42"-wide fabric.

Fabric	Pattern Pieces		
	Left panel	*Center panel*	*Right panel*
2 yards of dark-brown solid	7	6, 9	7
1¼ yards of pale-yellow-and-teal print #1	1, 4, 6	5, 7	3, 5
1 yard of pale yellow-and-teal print #2	5	4, 8	6
¾ yard of light-blue solid	3	1	2
½ yard of solid light-blue silk	2	—	1, 4
1 fat eighth (9" x 21") of solid red silk	9	—	9
1 fat eighth of solid yellow silk	8	2	8
Additional Materials			
1⅜ yards of fabric for facings			
3¾ yards of fabric for backings			
3 pieces, 24" x 45", of batting			

Preparing the Patterns

Refer to "Fast-Piece Appliqué Basics" on page 17.

1. Enlarge each of the panel patterns on page 73 to 19" x 40" (600% on a photocopy machine) using the desired method.

2. Use the full-sized patterns to make freezer-paper templates for each panel.

Assembling the Panels

Refer to "Fast-Piece Appliqué Basics" and the following instructions to construct each panel. Use the full-sized paper patterns for appliqué placement.

Left and Right Panels

1. Using the templates for the left panel, assemble the following pairs of pieces: 1 and 7, and 8 and 9.

2. Join the 1/7 piece to piece 2. Add piece 3 to this unit.

3. Join the 1–3/7 unit to piece 4. Add piece 5 to this unit.

4. Join the 1–5/7 unit to piece 6.

5. Refer to "Set-On Pieces" on page 23 to sew the 8/9 piece onto piece 5 of the assembled panel.

6. Remove the freezer-paper templates and trim the outermost fabrics to the stitching line.

7. Repeat steps 1–6 using the freezer-paper templates for the right panel.

Center Panel

1. Using the templates for the center panel, assemble the following pairs of pieces: 1 and 9, 2 and 3, and 4 and 6.

2. Join the 1/9 piece to the 2/3 piece.

3. Join the 4/6 piece to the 1–3/9 unit.

4. Join the 1–4/6/9 unit to piece 7. Add piece 5 to this unit.

5. Join the 1–7/9 unit to piece 8 to complete the panel.

6. Remove the freezer-paper templates and trim the outermost fabrics to the stitching line.

Finishing

Refer to "Finishing Details" on page 25.

1. Layer each panel with batting and backing; baste the layers together.

2. Add any desired couching and machine quilting details.

3. Trim each panel to 18½" x 39½".

4. Prepare and attach facing strips to the edges of each panel, but do not hand stitch them to the backing yet. I used facing rather than binding to give the illusion of connectivity between the panels when they're hung together.

5. Add any additional hand stitching and bead quilting.

6. Fold the facings to the back of each panel and hand stitch them in place.

Sweet Dreams
Enlarge pattern 600%.
Each panel size: 19" x 40"

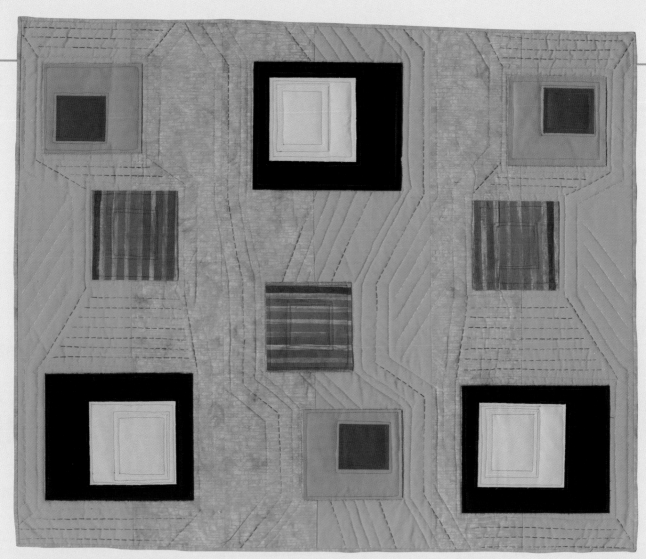

Finished quilt size: 45½" x 42"

Geometric Gems

As I started to create the designs for this book, I looked for items and images of scenes that I could simplify and modify to make fun and meaningful designs. Basic geometric shapes are some of my favorite forms to play with. Sometimes, just changing the sizes, or repeating, arranging, and rearranging surface-pattern ideas using just one simple shape can supply you with amazing designs for a quilt.

Traditional quilts often use squares repeated to create a multitude of patterns, so I thought I'd use squares a little bit differently in this quilt. I hope you enjoy the simplicity of these squares, but imagine what you could do with circles or triangles on their own. Think about all the possibilities.

I wanted the square, geometric gems to catch the eye of the viewer and stand out among a combination of machine-quilted and big-stitch hand-quilted secondary designs. To allow the simple gems ample opportunity to shine, I used my fused-fabric construction method.

Materials

In addition to the items listed in "Supplies" on page 10, you'll need the following materials. Yardage is based on 42"-wide fabric. The yardage listed for the appliqué pieces is enough for the fused-fabric backing.

Fabric	Pattern Pieces		
	Left panel	*Center panel*	*Right panel*
1 yard of medium-orange solid	Background	Background	Background
1 yard of pale-orange batik	Background	Background	Background
¾ yard of purple solid	6	6	6
¼ yard of red-and-orange stripe batik	3	3	3
¼ yard of medium-green solid	2	2	2
1 fat quarter (18" x 21") of pale-lavender solid	4	4	4
1 fat quarter of pale-green solid	5	5	5
1 fat quarter of fuchsia solid	1	1	1
Additional Materials			
½ yard of orange fabric for binding			
2⅔ yards of fabric for backing			
48" x 52" piece of batting			
1¾ yards of 17"-wide paper-backed fusible web for fused-fabric technique			

Preparing the Patterns

Refer to "Fast-Piece Appliqué Basics" on page 17.

1. Enlarge each of the panel patterns on page 77 to 16" x 42" (625% on a photocopy machine) using the desired method.

2. Use the full-sized patterns to make freezer-paper templates for each panel.

Preparing the Backgrounds and Appliqués

1. From the medium-orange solid, cut 3 strips, 10½" x 42".

2. From the pale-orange batik, cut 3 strips, 6½" x 42".

3. Sew each orange solid strip to an orange batik strip along the long edges. Press the seam allowances open.

4. Referring to the materials list and "Fused-Fabric Elements" on page 20, use the freezer-paper templates to prepare the appliqués. Create fused appliqué units from pieces 1 and 2, and pieces 4–6 on each panel.

Assembling the Quilt Top

1. Refer to "Set-On Pieces" on page 23 and the full-sized paper pattern to position, tape, and stitch one prepared 1/2 unit, 3 piece, and 4–6 unit on each of the three background panels, referring to the photo for the placement of the background fabrics on each panel.

2. Remove the freezer-paper templates and trim the outermost fabrics to the stitching line.

3. Trim each panel to 15½" x 42". Sew the panels together along the long edges.

Save the Scraps

Before preparing the quilt top for finishing, you may choose to cut away the excess fabric behind each of the appliquéd units. Because they were stitched onto the pieced background, the resulting scraps make great pieces to be used in another project.

Check out "Scrap Happy Pillow" by visiting ShopMartingale.com/extras for instructions on turning the scraps into a pillow.

Finishing

Refer to "Finishing Details" on page 25.

1. Layer the quilt top with batting and backing; baste the layers together.

2. Add any desired couching and machine quilting details.

3. Prepare and attach the binding but do not fold it to the back.

4. Add any additional hand stitching and bead quilting.

5. Fold the binding to the back of the quilt and hand stitch it in place.

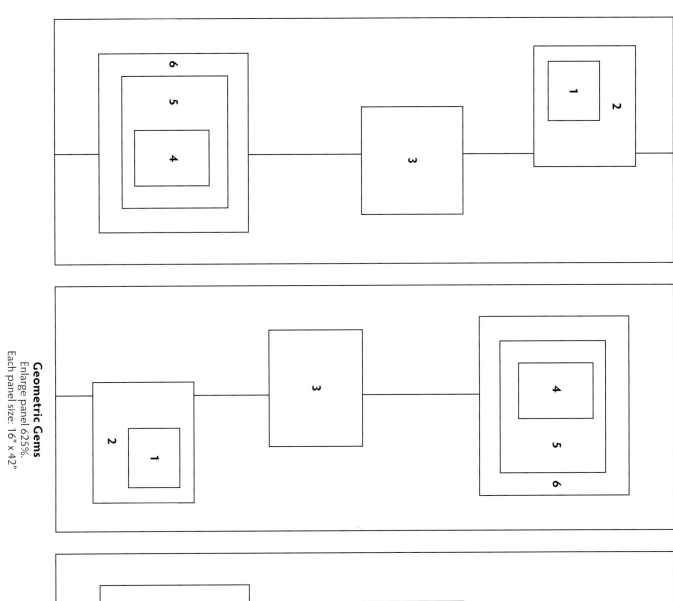

Geometric Gems
Enlarge panel 625%.
Each panel size: 16" x 42"

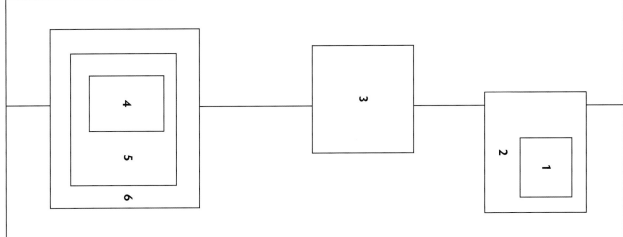

Resources

This list includes manufacturers, suppliers, and service providers for the materials and long-arm quilting provided for this book.

Manufacturers and Suppliers

Anthology Fabrics
800-450-2030
AnthologyFabrics.com

Hoffman California Fabrics
800-547-0100
HoffmanFabrics.com

Kreinik Manufacturing Company, Inc.
800-537-2166
Kreinik.com
info@kreinik.com

P&B Textiles
800-351-9087
PBTex.com

Robert Kaufman Fabrics
800-877-2066
RobertKaufman.com

Studio E Fabrics
800-294-9495
StudioEFabrics.com

Superior Threads
800-499-1777
SuperiorThreads.com

Therm O Web
800-323-0799
ThermoWebOnline.com

Weeks Dye Works, Inc.
877-OVERDYE (683-7393)
WeeksDyeWorks.com

Long-Arm Quilting Service Providers

Angela Walters
QuiltingIsMyTherapy.com
angelawaltersquilting@gmail.com

Cory Allender
435-229-5720
corycats25@gmail.com

Lisa Sipes
ThatCrazyQuiltyGirl.com
Lisa@thatcrazyquiltygirl.com

Maddie Ketray
BAQS
BadAssQuiltersSociety.com

Mandy Leins
Mandalei Quilts
Gansevoort, NY
Mandalei.com

Acknowledgments

Non-quilters are always surprised when you fill them in on what a wild ride quilting and writing can take you on. The journey is always changing and always challenging. Through it I've met the most amazing people and I feel really blessed to be able to once again give really big thanks to everyone who has made my journey of writing and sharing such a rewarding experience.

My family and California friends, now so far away since our move to Kentucky, are always just a phone call away and remain supportive in a very special way. The quilt world is big, but it always feels small. It was especially grand for me to reach out to some amazing long-arm quilters from all over when working on these quilts. Thanks to each of you: Maddie Ketray (Tennessee), Mandy Leins (New York), Cory Allender (Utah), Vicki Tymczyszyn (California), Angela Walters (Missouri), and Lisa Sipes (Pennsylvania).

Our move to Kentucky has been wonderful and there's now a whole new community that lent their expertise and time to helping me pull this book together. Big hugs to stunt binders Helen Davis, Valarie Pollard, Cathy Neri, and Michele Duffy. They were amazing and our stitching time together was a treat. As it came down to the wire, there were others that volunteered to help, but the snow kept them housebound, so a huge thank-you goes out to Kristin Williams who, during the last week leading up to deadline, braved the cold to step in to help with all the sample photography.

Thank you all.
~Rose

About the Author

Photo by Carlo Parducho

It was a warm, sunny day in Seattle when Rose Hughes fell in love with a quilt at the Folk Life Festival. She had no idea that quilts would soon offer her a wild and wonderful, artful journey that is still going strong after 20 years. During those years, Rose let her love of nature, photography, and art inspire her stitching journey. In this, her fourth book, she shares her love of simple graphic images and ways to quickly create a quilt top waiting for those beautiful quilting stitches, the same kind of stitches that kept pulling her back to that Folk Life Festival booth for another look at that quilt.

Rose loves to share her quilting passions. She travels the world, providing entertaining and educational lectures, and teaching on topics such as her Fast-Piece Appliqué method. Her line-up of workshops also includes design, fabric painting, color, and all forms of embellishment.

As Rose continues to pursue her own art, you may find her quilts in juried exhibitions throughout the world, and you may also click on the television or computer to find her sharing her work and methods. She enjoys membership in numerous quilt- and art-related organizations and finds joy in sharing her love of the art of quilting through her blog, RoseHughes.blogspot.com; her website, RoseHughes.com; and her Facebook page.